Nikon D850 User Guide

How to Use Your Camera with Step-by-Step Tutorials, Autofocus and Exposure, 4K Video Setup, and Troubleshooting Tips

Randy Osborn

shooting conditions, equipment variations, and personal skill level. Always exercise caution when handling camera equipment, accessories, and electronic devices, and follow the official Nikon D850 instruction manual for safety and operational procedures.

The author and publisher shall not be held liable for any direct, indirect, incidental, or consequential damages, injuries, or losses arising from the use or misuse of the information, suggestions, or recommendations provided in this book.

By reading this guide, you acknowledge that you are solely responsible for your choices, actions, and results when applying the content presented.

Dedication

To every photographer who has ever lifted a camera not just to take a picture, but to capture a feeling, a memory, or a fleeting moment of beauty.

This book is for the beginners who are brave enough to start, for the enthusiasts who refuse to stop learning, and for the professionals who remind us that mastery is a lifelong pursuit.

And most of all, it is dedicated to you—the reader—who believes that the Nikon D850 is more than a tool, but a gateway to telling your own story through images.

Table of Contents

How to Use This Book

Learning a camera as powerful as the Nikon D850 can feel like stepping into a cockpit full of buttons, switches, and endless options. This book was written to make that journey less intimidating, more practical, and far more enjoyable. Instead of overwhelming you with jargon or simply repeating the official manual, it is designed to be a *hands-on companion*—a guide you can dip into when you need clarity, inspiration, or a quick solution in the middle of a shoot.

Quick-Start Readers' Note

If you just unboxed your Nikon D850 and can't wait to start shooting, skip straight to Chapter 1: Getting Started Without Overwhelm. There, you'll find a step-by-step "day one" setup that will have you taking sharp, well-exposed photos within minutes. You don't need to read the entire book before picking up your camera—the guide is designed so you can learn as you shoot.

Think of it this way: start simple, get results right away, then circle back to the other chapters to unlock deeper features like custom buttons, advanced autofocus tracking, or 4K video setup.

How to Navigate the Book

- **Beginner Friendly:** Chapters are written in plain language, without assuming any prior technical knowledge. You can follow along even if the D850 is your very first DSLR.

- **Modular Design:** Each chapter is self-contained. If you're struggling with autofocus, jump to that section. If video is your main interest, head directly to the video chapter.

- **Scenario-Based Examples:** Settings and techniques are explained using real-world situations—family portraits, kids' soccer games, weddings, travel landscapes—so you always know when and why to use them.

Symbols, Tips & Cheat Sheets

Throughout the book, you'll notice small markers to make your learning faster and more practical:

- **Quick Tip:** Simple, actionable advice to try immediately.

- **Shortcut:** Time-saving button combinations or menu hacks that make the D850 faster to use.

- **Troubleshooting:** Solutions to common problems like blurry shots, battery drain, or confusing error messages.

- **Cheat Sheet:** One-page summaries that condense the key settings for specific scenarios (portraits, landscapes, action, low light). These are designed to be your quick reference before a shoot.

- **Pro Insight:** Real-world strategies and creative ideas drawn from professional photographers who rely on the D850 in demanding conditions.

Making the Most of This Guide

You don't need to memorize every setting or technique in one sitting. Photography is a skill best learned through *practice and repetition.* Keep your D850 close while you read, test the settings as you go, and don't be afraid to experiment. The more you interact with your camera alongside these pages, the more natural it will all feel.

Remember: *this book is not here to replace your creativity—it's here to remove the barriers so your creativity can shine.*

Preface

Discover the Ultimate Nikon D850 User Guide – Your Complete Companion for Stunning Photography and 4K Video

The *Nikon D850* is more than just a camera—it's an incredible tool for creative expression. But with its deep menus and professional-level features, getting the best out of it can feel overwhelming. That's where this Nikon D850 User Guide comes in. Written in plain language, this book is not just another dry *Nikon D850 manual*—it's a step by step tutorial designed to walk you through everything you need, from your very first shot to advanced techniques for pros.

Whether you're searching for a Nikon D850 for beginners book or a practical Nikon D850 camera guide, this resource delivers. Think of it as both a digital photography for beginners handbook and an advanced DSLR photography guide that grows with you. It combines Nikon photography tips, easy-to-follow lessons, and professional insights into one accessible Nikon D850 photography book.

Inside, you'll find:

- The best settings for Nikon D850, explained clearly so you can shoot with confidence in any situation.

- A full Nikon D850 tutorial covering autofocus, ISO, exposure, and real-world setups.

- A practical autofocus and exposure guide that shows you how to get sharp, perfectly lit images.

- A D850 video and 4K guide to help you unlock cinematic video quality, including audio setups and stabilization tips.

- Real examples: Nikon D850 landscape photography setup, a wedding photography guide, wildlife photography tips, and more.

- Troubleshooting sections on Nikon D850 autofocus and ISO settings, troubleshooting Nikon D850 problems, sensor cleaning, and memory card setup.

This is a complete guide to Nikon D850 photography. Whether you want to learn how to use Nikon D850 for portraits, try a step by step tutorial for landscapes, or follow a wedding photography workflow, the answers are here. You'll even find bonus tools like photography settings cheat sheets, lighting tips, and post-processing strategies in Capture One, Lightroom editing, and social media preparation.

Because photography is global, this book also acknowledges readers worldwide—whether you are looking for a Nikon D850 Handbuch, a Nikon D850 guía, or a Nikon D850 mode d'emploi, you'll find practical help here. It's a Nikon D850 guide book written for everyone, whether you bought your Nikon D850 new or found a trusted Nikon D850 used model.

Along the way, you'll also sharpen your fundamentals. From beginner photography basics to learning shutter speed, ISO, aperture, this book doubles as an understanding camera settings book. It's not just for Nikon—it compares with photography books for beginners DSLR, covers photography techniques, and even explains how settings relate to other gear, like Nikon point and shoot digital cameras or accessories.

You'll learn how to:

- Master portrait photography guides with natural and studio light.

- Refine your landscape setup with ND filters, tripods, and long exposure tricks.

- Elevate your wildlife photography with AF-C modes and telephoto lenses.

- Use creative photography lighting tips for both events and artistic projects.

- Prepare your files for print now camera labs, stock sites, and social media.

Unlike a dense camera handbook or a confusing technical manual, this photography settings guide book is designed for real photographers who want clarity, speed, and results. If you've ever looked for camera settings cheat sheets for Nikon or wondered about a camera user guide that truly simplifies things, this book delivers the same value for your D850.

No hype, no gimmicks—just a practical Nikon DSLR tutorial that helps you start shooting better today. With its focus on easy use camera setups, professional workflows, and guidance that balances inspiration with real technique, this book ensures your D850 feels like an awesome digital camera and not a puzzle box.

If you're ready to stop fumbling through menus, reduce mistakes, and unlock the full power of your D850—whether for portrait photography, weddings, wildlife, landscapes, or shooting video with Nikon D850—this is the photography setting guide you've been waiting for.

- Perfect for beginners, enthusiasts, and professionals.
- Includes cheat sheets for colors, exposure, and quick setups.
- Written as a complete Nikon photography, DSLR photography, and digital camera tutorial.

With this Nikon D850 tutorial and camera guide in hand, you'll not only master your camera—you'll master the art of photography itself.

Introduction

Why the Nikon D850 Still Matters

When Nikon first introduced the D850, it wasn't just another DSLR—it was a statement. With its 45.7-megapixel sensor, outstanding dynamic range, robust autofocus system, and 4K video capabilities, the D850 quickly earned a reputation as one of the greatest cameras Nikon has ever made. For many photographers, it became a dream camera, combining resolution, speed, and rugged build quality in a way that few other models could match.

Years later, in a world increasingly dominated by mirrorless technology, the Nikon D850 still holds a special place in the hearts of both professionals and passionate hobbyists. Wedding photographers praise it for its reliability and battery life, landscape shooters love the depth and richness of its files, and portrait photographers appreciate the sheer detail it can render. Beginners who make the leap to this model often feel as though they are stepping into professional territory, unlocking features they never imagined having at their fingertips.

The Legend of the D850

The Nikon D850 has been described as a "workhorse," a "legend," and even the "endgame DSLR." Why? Because it solved a problem that many cameras before it could not: how to balance ultra-high resolution with speed and performance. Most high-megapixel cameras at the time were slow and limited to studio or tripod use. The D850 shattered that mold. It offered a massive sensor *and* the ability to shoot action, wildlife, and events without compromise.

For photographers who wanted a single body that could handle weddings on Saturday, landscapes on Sunday, and commercial shoots during the week, the D850 became indispensable. Its reputation was built not only on specs, but on trust—it delivers consistent results, no matter the conditions.

DSLR vs Mirrorless: Where the D850 Shines Today

There is no denying that mirrorless cameras like Nikon's Z8 and Z9 are changing the industry. They bring faster burst rates, electronic viewfinders, and advanced autofocus tracking that DSLR systems can't always match. Yet, despite this shift, the D850 continues to stand tall.

Why? Because it offers advantages that still matter:

- **Battery life:** The optical viewfinder draws almost no power, allowing thousands of shots per charge—something mirrorless shooters often envy.

- **Rugged build:** The magnesium alloy body is a tank, weather-sealed to handle rain, dust, and the rigors of professional work.

- **Optical viewfinder experience:** Many photographers still prefer the clarity and immediacy of looking directly through glass rather than a digital display.

- **Lens ecosystem:** With decades of Nikon F-mount lenses available, from affordable classics to high-end glass, the D850 offers unmatched flexibility without forcing expensive upgrades.

- **Value longevity:** For those who don't need the very latest mirrorless tech, the D850 remains one of the most cost-effective ways to get professional image quality that rivals much newer systems.

In short, while mirrorless is the future, the D850 remains a powerhouse in the present—especially for those who prize reliability, versatility, and image quality above all else.

What This Guide Gives You That the Official Manual Doesn't

If you've ever opened the Nikon D850's official manual, you know it's thorough—sometimes *too* thorough. It tells you what every button does, but rarely explains *when* or *why* you should use it. It lists settings, but doesn't show you how they fit into real-life shooting situations. For many, the manual feels more like a technical reference than a learning tool.

That's where this guide is different. This book is designed to be your bridge between technical possibility and creative reality. Inside these pages, you'll find:

- **Plain-language explanations** of complex settings.

- **Scenario-based examples** that show you exactly which setup works best for portraits, sports, landscapes, or video.

- **Quick cheat sheets** you can reference before a shoot, so you spend less time digging through menus and more time capturing moments.

- **Troubleshooting tips** to solve common problems—whether it's soft focus, noisy images, or confusing error messages.

- **Professional insights** to help you grow beyond the beginner stage and tap into the D850's full potential.

This is not just a manual; it's a companion. My goal is that as you read, you'll feel less like you're studying a piece of equipment and more like you're having a conversation with a fellow photographer who's been there, made the mistakes, and found the solutions.

So whether you are unboxing your D850 for the first time or you've owned it for years but never ventured beyond Auto mode, this book will guide you step by step. By the end, you won't just understand your camera—you'll trust it, and more importantly, you'll trust yourself to create with it.

Chapter 1

Getting Started Without Overwhelm

Unboxing a Nikon D850 is both exciting and a little intimidating. You're holding a camera that professionals have called legendary, a body packed with features and possibilities. But at this moment, all you really want is to get started without feeling buried under buttons, menus, and technical jargon. That's exactly what this chapter is for.

Rather than throwing you into the deep end, we'll walk through the essentials step by step—setting up the camera for the very first time, preparing your batteries and memory cards, attaching a lens, and taking your very first photo. Think of this as your "Day-One" roadmap. By the time you finish this chapter, you'll have captured your first sharp, well-exposed image with confidence.

Unboxing and First Setup

When you open the box, you'll find the Nikon D850 body, a rechargeable EN-EL15a battery, a charger, a strap, and a few other small accessories. Here's how to set things up right away:

1. **Charge the Battery**

   Before anything else, place the EN-EL15a battery into the charger and plug it in. A full charge ensures you won't run out of power mid-shoot. A fully charged battery on the D850 can easily get you through a long day of shooting, so starting with 100% is worth the wait.

2. **Insert the Battery and Memory Cards**

   Open the compartment on the bottom of the camera and slide in the charged battery until it clicks. On the right-hand side of the body, open the card slot cover. The D850 takes two types of memory cards: XQD (or CFexpress Type B with updated firmware) and SD cards (UHS-II recommended).

o Use an XQD or CFexpress card if you plan to shoot a lot of high-resolution RAW or 4K video.

o Use a fast SD card if you're just starting and want something affordable.

Slide the card in with the label facing the back of the camera until it clicks into place.

3. **Attach a Lens**

Remove the body cap from the D850 and the rear cap from your lens. Align the white dot on the lens with the white dot on the camera mount, then twist gently clockwise until it locks. Always keep the lens release button in mind for later—press and twist counter-clockwise to remove.

4. **Turn the Camera On**

Flip the power switch around the shutter button. You'll see the top LCD light up and the viewfinder activate. Congratulations—you've powered up your D850 for the first time.

The Quick-Start Beginner Setup

The Nikon D850 is capable of more customization than most people will ever use. But on day one, you don't need everything—you just need a foundation that will let you shoot right away without frustration. Here's the setup I recommend for beginners:

- **Auto ISO:** Let the camera adjust ISO automatically for you. This keeps images bright enough without you worrying about noise.

- **Aperture Priority (A mode):** Turn the mode dial to "A." This setting allows you to control depth of field (how blurry or sharp the background looks) while the camera sets the shutter speed.

- **Picture Control: Standard:** In the Shooting Menu, set Picture Control to "Standard." It gives natural colors and contrast without going overboard.

- **White Balance: Auto:** Leave it on Auto for now—the D850 does an excellent job of guessing the lighting.

- **Focus Mode: AF-S (Single Servo) for still subjects.**
  Perfect for portraits or objects that aren't moving much.

- **Focus Area: Single Point AF.** This allows you to place the focus point exactly where you want sharpness.

These few settings alone will simplify your early shooting experience while still letting you feel the D850's power.

Step-by-Step: Your First Sharp, Well-Exposed Shot

Now let's put it all into practice:

1. **Hold the Camera Properly**

   Grip the camera firmly with your right hand, wrapping your fingers around the grip. Use your left hand to support the lens from underneath. Pull the camera gently against your face for stability. This reduces blur from hand-shake.

2. **Turn the Mode Dial to "A"** (Aperture Priority).

This means you'll set the f-stop, and the camera will handle

shutter speed.

3. **Set Your Aperture**

Rotate the front dial near the shutter button. For a portrait of

a person, try f/2.8 or f/4 (blurry background). For a

landscape, try f/8 or f/11 (sharp front to back).

4. **Compose the Shot**

Look through the viewfinder, move the focus point using the

multi-selector, and place it over your subject's eye or the part

of the scene you want sharp.

5. **Half-Press the Shutter**

The camera will focus and meter the light. You'll hear a

small beep and see the focus indicator in the viewfinder

confirm focus.

6. **Fully Press the Shutter**

Capture your first image. The D850 will handle shutter speed and ISO for you while giving you creative control over depth of field.

7. **Review Your Photo**

Press the playback button to check sharpness and exposure. Use the zoom buttons to check details. If it's blurry, try raising your ISO or holding the camera steadier. If it's too dark or bright, use the exposure compensation button (+/-) to adjust and reshoot.

That's it—your first confident shot with the D850.

Cheat Sheet: D850 "Day-One" Setup

To make things even easier, here's a quick recap of the recommended first-day settings:

- **Mode:** Aperture Priority (A)

- **ISO:** Auto (with a range from 100 to 6400)

- **Aperture:** f/2.8–f/4 for portraits, f/8–f/11 for landscapes

- **White Balance:** Auto

- **Picture Control:** Standard

- **Focus Mode:** AF-S (Single Servo)

- **Focus Area:** Single Point AF

- **Drive Mode:** Single Shot

Keep these in mind, and you'll have a simple yet powerful foundation for your photography journey.

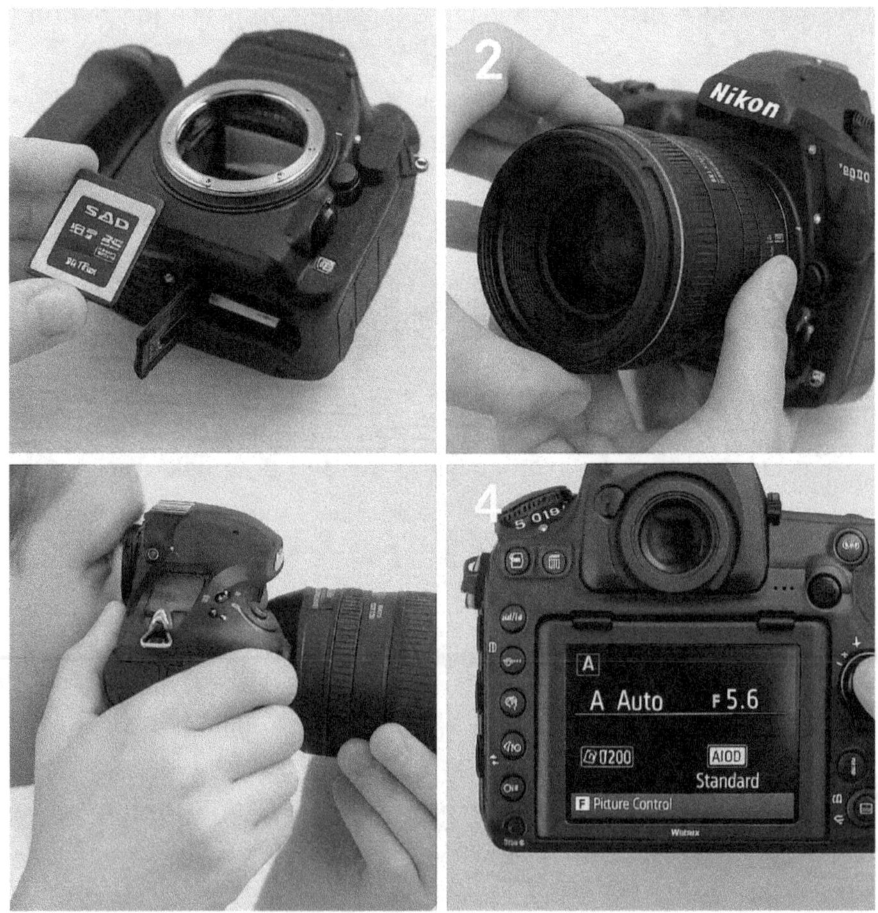

Chapter 2

Navigating Menus & Custom Settings Without Confusion

If Chapter 1 was about simply getting your Nikon D850 up and running, this chapter is about making it feel like *your* camera. The D850 has one of the deepest and most customizable menu systems Nikon has ever created. While that's a blessing for fine-tuning every detail, it can also feel overwhelming at first. Many new owners confess that half the time they don't know where a setting is hidden or why it even matters.

The good news is you don't need to memorize every menu option or read through a thick manual. You only need to understand the core menus, know which settings are worth adjusting right away, and then learn how to create shortcuts so the camera bends to your style of shooting.

Let's strip the menus down to plain English and show you how to master them without confusion.

The Deep Nikon Menu Explained in Plain English

When you press the *Menu* button on the back of your D850, you'll see a vertical list of colored icons. Each one represents a different category:

- **Playback Menu (blue icon):** Controls how your images are displayed after you shoot them. You can delete, protect, or set up slideshows here.

- **Photo Shooting Menu (green icon):** The heart of your still photography controls. File type (RAW/JPEG), image quality, ISO settings, and Picture Controls live here.

- **Movie Shooting Menu (also green, with a film strip symbol):** Similar to the photo menu, but specific to video recording—resolution, frame rates, and audio controls.

- **Custom Settings Menu (pencil icon):** This is where you fine-tune autofocus, exposure, timers, buttons, and behaviors. Think of it as the personalization hub.

- **Setup Menu (wrench icon):** General housekeeping—time, date, language, format memory card, firmware version.

- **Retouch Menu (paintbrush icon):** Allows you to do light editing in-camera. It's more of a novelty—serious editing belongs in software like Lightroom.

- **My Menu (star icon):** A customizable menu where you can place your most-used options for quick access.

Once you know these categories, the system feels less like a maze and more like organized folders.

Essential Settings You Must Change Right

Away

When you first turn on the D850, it's set to Nikon's defaults. Some are fine, but others will slow you down or limit your image quality. Here are the settings worth changing immediately:

1. **Image Quality to RAW or RAW+JPEG.** This unlocks the full potential of the 45.7MP sensor. If you're new to editing, use RAW+JPEG so you get a ready-to-share JPEG and a RAW file for later.

2. **ISO Sensitivity Settings → Auto ISO.** Turn this on with a maximum ISO cap (say 6400) and minimum shutter speed. It keeps your exposures consistent while preventing overly noisy images.

3. **Picture Control to Standard or Neutral.** Vibrant or Vivid may oversaturate colors. Standard gives you a natural base, Neutral works best if you plan to edit.

4. **AF-C Priority Selection to Release + Focus.** This balances sharpness and speed when tracking moving subjects.

5. **Custom Setting: Back-Button Focus.** Assign autofocus to the AF-ON button, freeing the shutter button just for taking the shot. This prevents refocusing every time you press the shutter halfway.

6. **Set Date, Time, and File Naming.** Simple, but if you forget this, your images will all have generic names that become a nightmare to organize later.

Customizing the "My Menu" Tab for Your Style of Shooting

The "My Menu" tab is one of the most underrated features on the D850. Instead of digging through endless submenus, you can place your most-used options in one quick list.

Here's how to make it practical:

- Add **ISO Sensitivity Settings** so you can quickly adjust Auto ISO range.

- Add **Format Memory Card** so you can clear your card before a shoot without hunting through Setup.

- Add **Image Area** (FX vs DX crop). Switching to DX crop is handy for wildlife if you want more reach.

- Add **White Balance** if you often switch between indoor and outdoor shooting.

- Add **Focus Mode/AF-Area Mode** for fast changes between portraits and action.

Over time, refine this list to fit your habits. A portrait photographer's My Menu will look different from a wildlife shooter's. The beauty is that *your* essentials are always one button away.

How to Save and Recall Shooting Banks (U1/U2 Custom Profiles)

One of the most powerful ways to simplify the D850 is to save entire sets of preferences into what Nikon calls *Shooting Banks*. Think of them as user profiles. Instead of changing settings every time you switch from landscapes to action, you can store your preferred

sctups and rccall thcm instantly.

For example:

- **Bank A (Landscape):** Aperture Priority, ISO 64 base, Neutral Picture Control, Auto White Balance, AF-S Single Point.

- **Bank B (Action):** Shutter Priority, Auto ISO with high cap, Group-Area AF, Vivid Picture Control, Continuous High drive mode.

- **Bank C (Portraits):** Aperture Priority at f/2.8, Standard Picture Control, AF-S Single Point with Eye Focus, RAW+JPEG.

Once stored, you can flip between these banks in seconds, letting the camera adapt to your subject instead of you fiddling through menus.

Cheat Sheet: 10 Menu Hacks Every D850 User

Should Know

1. Assign ISO to the front dial for quick sensitivity changes without menus.

2. Use "My Menu" for instant access to your top five settings.

3. Enable Auto ISO with a minimum shutter speed linked to focal length—no more blurry telephoto shots.

4. Turn on grid lines in the display for straighter horizons.

5. Save custom Shooting Banks for portraits, landscapes, and sports.

6. Use Back-Button Focus to separate focus from the shutter button.

7. Add "Format Memory Card" to My Menu to speed up pre-shoot setup.

8. Set File Naming with your initials to avoid mixing cards with other photographers.

9. Enable Highlight Display ("zebra stripes") to prevent blown-out whites.

10. Customize function buttons (Fn1, Fn2) for features you want

instant access to, like depth of field preview or bracketing.

By now, you should feel less like the D850's menu is a locked vault

and more like it's a set of tools laid out on your workbench. The

more you set it up to match your habits, the less you'll think about

buttons and settings during a shoot. Instead, you'll stay focused on

what really matters—the image in front of you.

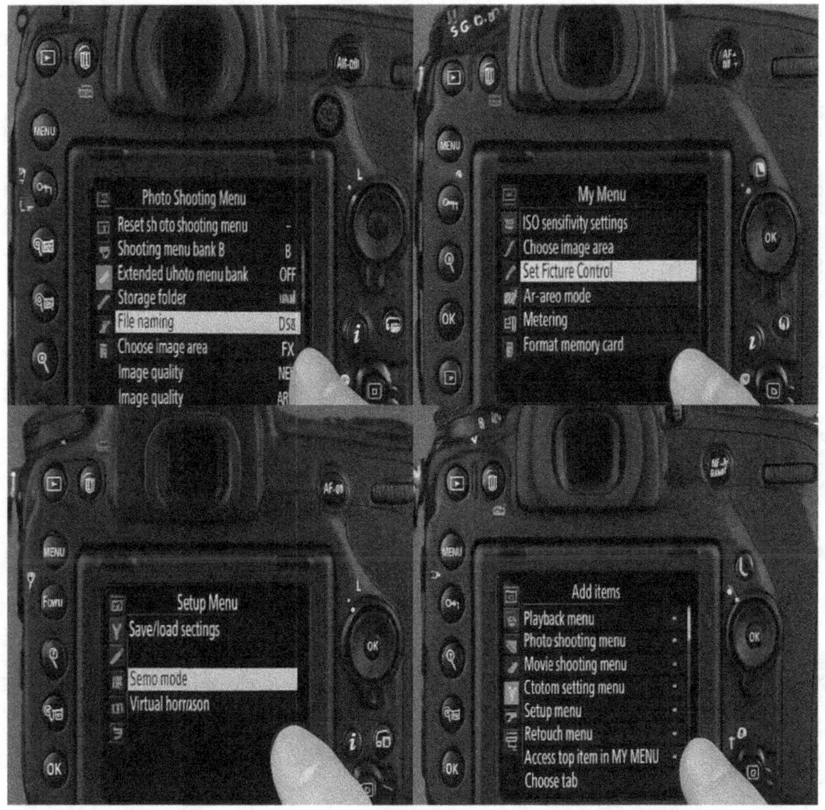

Chapter 3

Mastering Autofocus for Every Subject

If the Nikon D850 feels like a rocket ship, autofocus is the engine room. Get this right and everything else becomes easier—exposure, composition, even editing. The goal of this chapter is simple: demystify the 153-point AF system, show you exactly which mode to use and when, and give you fail-safe routines for portraits, sports, macro, and real-world chaos like kids running toward you.

Understanding the 153-Point AF System (in plain language)

The D850 uses a dedicated phase-detect autofocus module with 153 selectable points spread across the central area of the frame. Think of these points as little "grab spots" your camera can lock onto.

Some of them are cross-type points (extra sensitive to detail and contrast). The center cluster is the most reliable in low light; points near the edges work well but can hesitate in dim conditions.

Two big ideas to hold onto:

1. **AF mode = how the camera behaves over time.**

   o **AF-S (Single-Servo):** Locks focus once and stays put until you lift your finger. Best for still subjects.

   o **AF-C (Continuous-Servo):** Keeps refocusing as your subject moves. Best for action and anything unpredictable.

2. **AF-area mode = how many points the camera uses and who "chooses" the point.**
   You decide whether you want one specific point, a small cluster, a big cluster, or to hand the choice to the camera.

Once you separate *mode* (AF-S vs AF-C) from *area* (Single, Dynamic, Group, Auto, 3D), the system stops feeling mysterious.

When to Use Each AF-Area Mode

Single-Point AF

You choose one point and place it exactly where you want sharpness—an eye in a portrait, a lock on a landscape.

Use when: The subject isn't moving much and precision matters.

Pair with: AF-S for still life and posed portraits, AF-C for slow movers.

Dynamic-Area AF (9 / 25 / 72 / 153)

You pick a primary point; if the subject drifts off that point, the surrounding points help maintain focus.

Use when: The subject moves in a somewhat predictable path (a runner along a track, a bird gliding).

Which size?

- **9-point:** Small, precise (close-ups, modest movement).

- **25-point:** Versatile default for general action.

- **72- or 153-point:** Erratic or fast subjects that are hard to keep centered.

Group-Area AF

A tight cluster acts as one intelligent point, prioritizing the nearest subject within the group.

Use when: You need reliable focus on something moving toward you (brides walking the aisle, kids sprinting, dogs charging).

Strength: Stickiness and simplicity—less aiming precision required than single-point.

Auto-Area AF

The camera scans the scene and chooses points for you.

Use when: You have no time to select a point (spontaneous moments) or when using face detection in Live View.

Caution: It can grab the wrong subject if the scene is busy or your background is high contrast.

You select a starting point; the camera then tracks that subject across points as it moves around the frame.

Use when: The subject moves unpredictably side-to-side and you want to recompose freely—dancers, kids weaving through a crowd.

Tip: Works best with good light and a distinct subject color/contrast relative to the background.

Portrait AF vs Sports AF vs Macro AF (ready-to-use setups)

Portrait AF (posed or gently moving)

- **Mode:** AF-S for posed, AF-C for candid movement.

- **Area:** Single-Point for precision on the near eye; Group-Area if subject moves toward you.

- **Technique:** Place the point over the near eye; refocus every time the subject or you shift.

- **Extras:** Use a shutter speed of 1/125–1/250 to dodge subtle subject movement. If shooting wide open (f/1.8–f/2.8), be extra precise—depth of field is razor thin.

Sports / Wildlife AF

- **Mode:** AF-C (non-negotiable).

- **Area:** Start with Dynamic-Area 25 for lateral motion; switch to Group-Area for subjects coming at you; try 3D-Tracking when you want to keep a runner or bird in the frame while recomposing.

- **Technique:** Pan smoothly, keep your subject under the cluster, and use burst shooting.

- **Shutter speed:** Aim for 1/1000–1/2000 (faster for birds in flight).

- **ISO:** Let Auto ISO float with a cap you trust for your noise tolerance.

- **Mode:** AF-S for deliberate focus; AF-C if wind or subject sway is a factor.

- **Area: Single-Point**—you need surgical precision.

- **Technique:** Rock your body gently forward/back to land the plane of focus exactly where you want it. Consider Live View + magnification for pinpoint accuracy.

- **Shutter speed:** Use a tripod or raise shutter/ISO; tiny movements create huge focus shifts at macro distances.

Back-Button Focus (BBF) Explained Simply

By default, half-pressing the shutter focuses and fully pressing takes the photo. Back-Button Focus moves focusing to the AF-ON button under your right thumb. Why it's brilliant:

- You can focus once and recompose without the camera refocusing.

- In AF-C, you can track continuously while your shutter button only shoots—no accidental refocus.

- It stops that annoying hunting when you breathe on the shutter half-press.

How to set it up (typical steps on the D850):

1. In the Custom Settings (pencil icon), assign AF-ON to activate autofocus.

2. Disable focus on the shutter half-press (Shutter/AF-ON setting).

3. Practice: Hold AF-ON with your thumb to focus, release to lock, press shutter to take the shot. After a day, you won't go back.

Troubleshooting Soft or Missed Focus

When images aren't sharp, don't guess—diagnose.

1. **Shutter speed too slow.**

   If the subject or your hands are moving, you'll see blur even with perfect AF. Use the "1 over focal length" rule as a minimum (e.g., 1/200s for a 200mm lens) and go faster for action.

2. **Wrong AF-area mode.**

   Single-Point for precision, Group or Dynamic for movement, 3D when you need tracking across the frame. If the camera keeps grabbing the background, simplify to Single-Point or Group.

3. **Focus point on the wrong spot.**

   The D850's viewfinder doesn't have modern eye-AF. You must actively place the point over the near eye for portraits. Practice moving the point with the multi-selector without taking your eye off the finder.

4. **Low contrast or low light.**

   AF struggles on flat, dark surfaces. Aim for edges, textures, or switch to the center cluster. Use an AF-assist light or increase ambient light when possible.

5. **Subject too small in the frame.**

Give the AF system enough detail to lock. Zoom in, step closer, or use a tighter cluster (Group-Area).

6. **Lens switches and stabilization.**

Confirm the lens AF/MF switch is on AF. If you're using VR/IS on a tripod, try turning stabilization off to prevent feedback blur.

7. **Lens or body miscalibration.**

If front- or back-focus persists with multiple lenses, run AF Fine-Tune on the D850 to micro-adjust. Use a proper target and steady support.

8. **Diopter set wrong.**

If the viewfinder itself looks fuzzy, adjust the diopter wheel next to the eyepiece—this doesn't affect image focus but affects your ability to judge it.

9. **Depth of field too thin.**

At f/1.8 a slight sway moves the plane of focus off the eye. Stop down to f/2.8–f/4 for portraits unless you *need* razor-thin blur.

10. **Dirty contacts or filters.**

Clean lens/camera contacts carefully. Over-strong or poor-quality filters can degrade AF and sharpness; test without them.

Case Studies (step-by-step)

1) Wedding Portraits (natural light)

Goal: Crisp eyes, flattering depth of field, gentle skin tones.

Setup:

- AF mode AF-S (posed) or AF-C (candid).

- **Single-Point** on the near eye; use Group-Area if the subject is walking toward you.

- Aperture f/2.8–f/3.5, shutter 1/200–1/400, Auto ISO.

- **Back-Button Focus** on AF-ON.

Flow: Place the point on the eye, focus with AF-ON, recompose slightly for framing, shoot in short bursts to beat blinks. If the subject starts moving, switch to AF-C and Group-Area for stickier focus.

2) Birds in Flight

Goal: Lock focus on a fast, erratic subject against messy backgrounds.

Setup:

- **AF-C** mandatory.

- Start with Group-Area for head-on approaches; try Dynamic-Area 25 or 72 for lateral flight.

- Shutter 1/2000 or faster; Auto ISO; continuous high burst.

- Use a wide stance or monopod; track with smooth pans.

  Flow: Acquire with Group-Area, half-or back-button to lock, then track through the frame and keep firing as the bird crosses backgrounds. If the system slips to the background, release focus, reacquire on the subject, and continue.

3) Kids Running Toward You

Goal: Keep focus nailed on the face during unpredictable movement.

Setup:

- **AF-C** with Group-Area or Dynamic-Area 25.

- Shutter 1/1000–1/1600, Auto ISO, continuous high burst.

- BBF enabled so refocusing is constant while you shoot.

  Flow: Kneel to their eye level, fill more of the frame than you think, keep the AF cluster over the face, and fire short bursts as they close the distance. Review a few frames—if focus is landing on the chest, raise the cluster slightly to the face or stop down to f/4 for more depth.

Practical Drills (fast mastery)

- **Point-change drill:** With the camera to your eye, move the focus point from center to each corner without looking at your thumb. Do it daily for a week.

- **Mode-swap drill:** Photograph a moving subject twice—once with Dynamic-Area 25, once with Group-Area—and compare hit rate. Keep notes; pick your default.

- **Low-light drill:** In a dim room, practice acquiring focus on high-contrast edges with the center points. Learn what the camera likes.

Takeaway

Autofocus on the D850 isn't magic—it's a set of behaviors you choose on purpose. Pick the right *mode* (AF-S vs AF-C), match the *area* to the movement (Single for precision, Group/Dynamic for action, 3D for cross-frame tracking), and anchor your technique with back-button focus. Add a fast enough shutter and a little practice, and the camera will reward you with tack-sharp frames in situations that used to feel impossible.

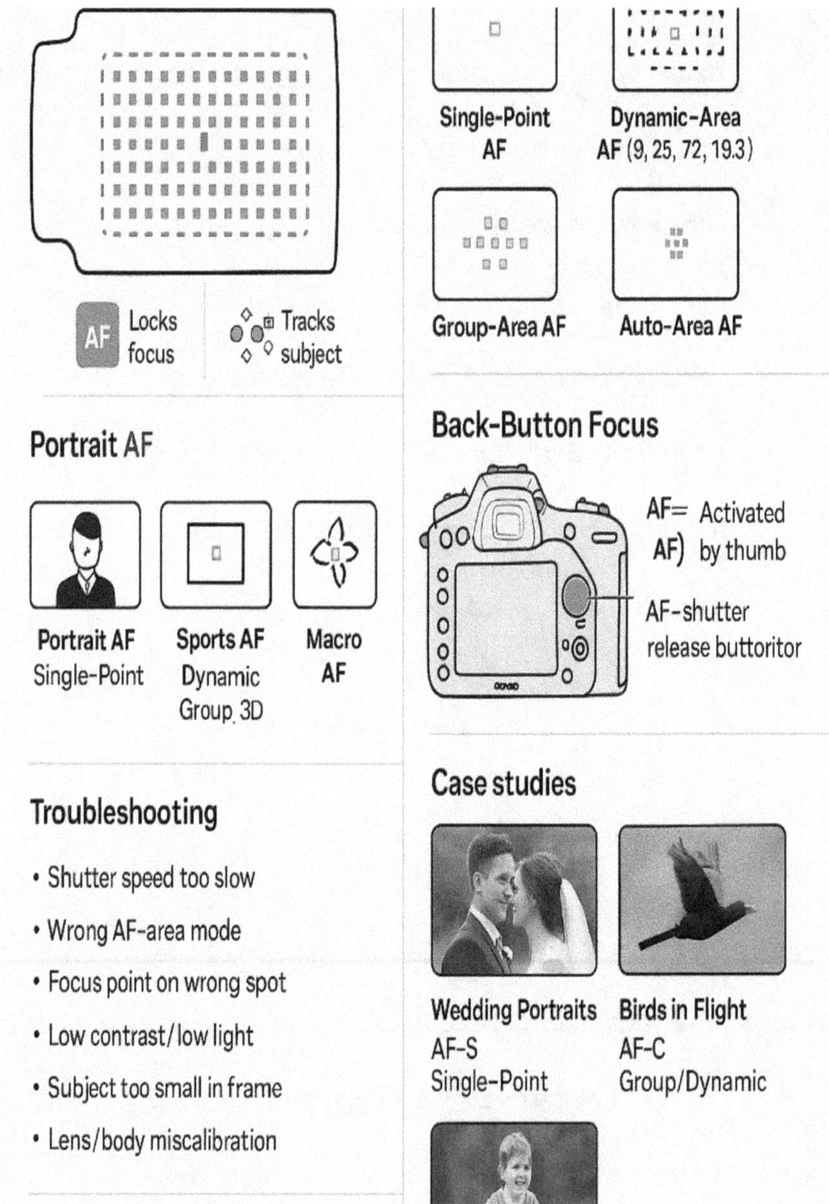

Chapter 4

Exposure & Image Quality Secrets

Sharp focus is only part of the equation. To create photographs that truly stand out, you need to understand how light interacts with your camera's sensor. Exposure and image quality are where the Nikon D850 really shows its muscle. Its full-frame, 45.7-megapixel sensor can deliver breathtaking files—but only if you learn to control it.

This chapter will help you step out of Auto mode with confidence, master the three building blocks of exposure, unlock the D850's enormous dynamic range, and make smart choices about file types. You'll also learn how to handle those massive RAW files without turning your computer into a snail.

Getting Out of Auto Mode Without Fear

Auto mode can feel safe—it chooses shutter speed, aperture, ISO, and even white balance for you. But Auto doesn't know your creative intent. Do you want a creamy background blur in a portrait? Do you want a waterfall to look silky smooth, or frozen in midair? Auto can't answer those questions.

The good news is that you don't have to jump straight to full Manual. Start with the semi-automatic modes that give you creative control while the D850 fills in the gaps:

- **Aperture Priority (A mode):** You control aperture, the camera sets shutter speed. Perfect for portraits, landscapes, and general shooting.

- **Shutter Priority (S mode):** You set the shutter speed, the camera sets aperture. Great for freezing action or adding motion blur.

- **Manual (M mode) with Auto ISO:** You set both aperture and shutter speed, and let the camera handle ISO to maintain exposure. Ideal when you want total control but still need flexibility.

Think of Auto as training wheels. Aperture Priority and Shutter Priority are like learning to steer, and Manual with Auto ISO is the balance point—freedom with safety net.

Understanding Aperture, Shutter Speed, ISO (Real-World Terms)

These three settings form the exposure triangle. Here's how to think about them in plain language:

- **Aperture (the "window size"):**
  Imagine your lens as a window. A wide aperture (f/1.8, f/2.8) is like opening the window wide—lots of light gets in, but the background blurs beautifully. A narrow aperture (f/8, f/11, f/16) is like a small crack—less light, but more of the

scene stays sharp.

Use wide apertures for portraits, narrow ones for landscapes.

- **Shutter Speed (the "curtain speed"):**

Think of the shutter as a curtain that opens and closes. Fast shutter speeds (1/1000s, 1/2000s) freeze action—a bird mid-flight, a child jumping. Slow shutter speeds (1/10s, 1s, 30s) blur motion—a waterfall becomes silky, night traffic turns into light trails.

Use fast speeds for sports, slow speeds for creative effects or low light.

- **ISO (the "sensor sensitivity"):**

ISO tells the sensor how sensitive to light it should be. Low ISO (64–200) gives the cleanest images with no grain. Higher ISO (3200–12800) brightens dim scenes but introduces noise.

Use low ISO when possible, raise it only when you need light.

Balance is everything. For example, if you open the aperture wide for a portrait, you'll need a faster shutter speed to avoid overexposure. If you slow the shutter for a waterfall, you may need to close down the aperture or lower ISO.

Dynamic Range: Capturing Shadows and Highlights

One of the Nikon D850's superpowers is dynamic range—the ability to capture detail in both deep shadows and bright highlights in the same shot. This is what allows you to shoot a dramatic sunrise without losing the detail in the foreground rocks, or photograph a bride in a white dress standing against a dark church wall without blowing out the highlights.

To harness it:

- **Shoot RAW.** RAW files preserve maximum detail in highlights and shadows.

- **Expose for the highlights.** If you're torn, it's safer to protect the bright areas. Shadows can often be recovered in editing; blown-out highlights are gone forever.

- **Use the Highlight Display ("blinkies").** Turn this on in playback to see flashing areas where highlights are overexposed.

- **Consider bracketing.** The D850 allows exposure bracketing—take multiple exposures at different settings, then blend them for a perfect balance.

Dynamic range is like having extra safety nets. Even if your photo looks a little dark straight out of the camera, you can often recover those details later.

How to Manage 45.7MP RAW Files Without

Slowing Your Computer

Each D850 RAW file can be upwards of 90 MB. That's a gift for detail, but a curse for your hard drive if you're unprepared. Here's how to stay efficient:

- **Use fast cards.** An XQD or CFexpress card handles large files much faster than SD.

- **Cull early.** Don't keep every frame. Review on the camera or use software like Photo Mechanic to select keepers before importing.

- **External storage.** Use portable SSDs or desktop hard drives to offload and organize. Keep working drives separate from backups.

- **Smart previews.** In Lightroom, build smart previews for faster editing without taxing your system with full RAWs constantly.

- **Shoot RAW + JPEG only when needed.** If you don't need instant JPEGs, stick with RAW to reduce space demands.

- **Compressed RAW.** Nikon offers "Lossless Compressed RAW." Use it—it reduces file size significantly without sacrificing quality.

Treat RAW files like fine art negatives: store them safely, but don't weigh yourself down with clutter.

JPEG vs RAW vs TIFF — When to Use Which

- **JPEG:**

  Small file, instantly shareable, baked-in processing by the camera (color, contrast, sharpening). Great for social media, quick client previews, or when you don't want to edit. But you sacrifice flexibility—if highlights are blown or shadows are muddy, they're harder to fix.

- **RAW (NEF for Nikon):**

  The digital negative. All sensor data is preserved, giving you maximum flexibility in editing—exposure, white balance, colors. Larger files, but the D850's full quality shines here.

Ideal for professional work, landscapes, portraits, and any image you want to perfect later.

- **TIFF:**

Gigantic, uncompressed files. Useful in professional print workflows where every detail matters, or when exporting for graphic designers. Rarely needed straight out of camera—most photographers edit in RAW and export to TIFF only at the end.

Rule of thumb: Shoot RAW for quality, JPEG when speed matters, TIFF only for final professional print or design needs.

Cheat Sheet: Exposure Settings for Common Scenarios

- **Portraits:** Aperture f/2.8–f/4 for background blur; shutter 1/125–1/250 to freeze subtle movement; ISO Auto with max at 3200.

- **Landscapes:** Aperture f/8–f/11 for depth; shutter varies (use tripod if slow); ISO 64 for maximum quality.

- **Sports/Action:** Shutter 1/1000–1/2000; aperture f/4–f/5.6 for balance; Auto ISO up to 6400.

- **Low Light Indoors:** Aperture f/1.8–f/2.8 if lens allows; shutter 1/100–1/200; Auto ISO up to 6400 or 12800 if needed.

- **Night Sky (Astro):** Aperture wide open (f/2.8 or faster); shutter 15–25 seconds; ISO 1600–3200; RAW mandatory.

- **Creative Motion Blur:** Shutter 1/10s or slower; aperture adjusted for exposure; tripod or steady hand essential.

Closing Thought

The Nikon D850 rewards photographers who take control of exposure. Don't be afraid to step away from Auto—each time you adjust aperture, shutter, or ISO with intention, you shape the image instead of letting the camera decide for you. Combine that with the

D850's extraordinary sensor, and you'll capture not just pictures, but photographs that hold detail, depth, and meaning.

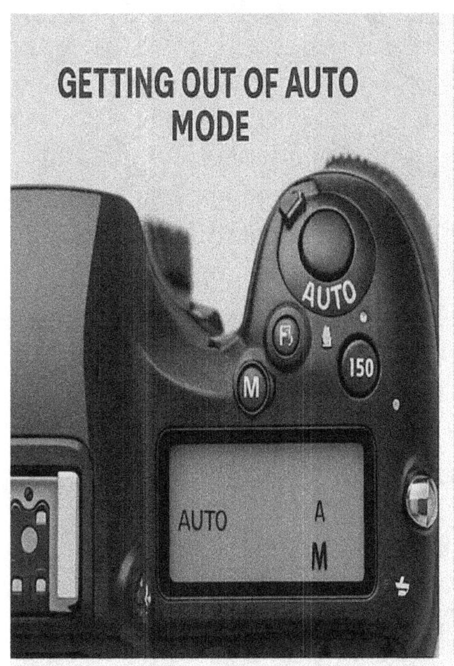

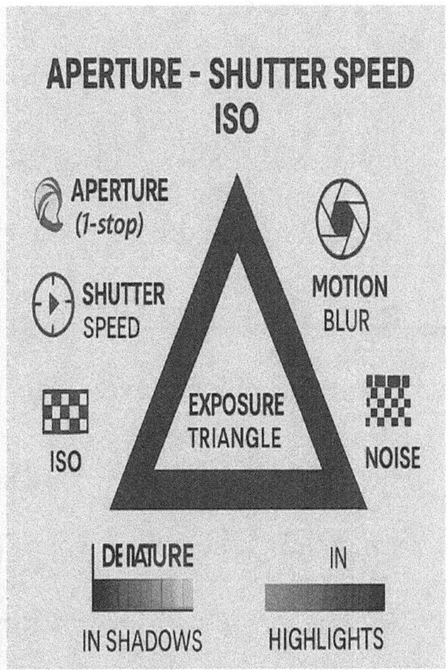

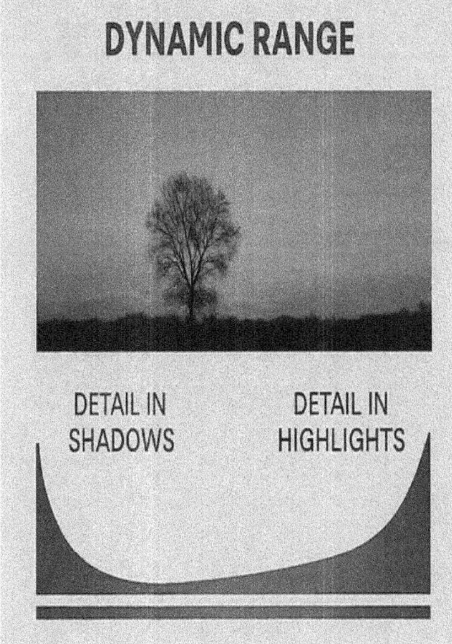

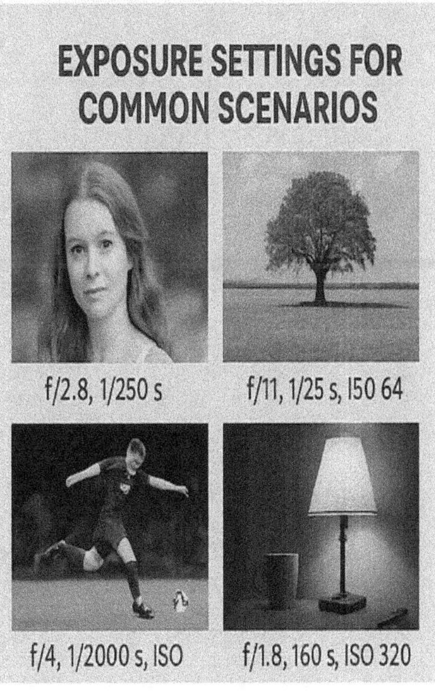

Chapter 5

Shooting in Low Light & Fast Action

The Nikon D850 isn't just a daytime powerhouse. With its full-frame sensor and impressive ISO range, it's built to handle the extremes—dimly lit interiors, nighttime streets, concerts, or sports where the action moves faster than your eyes can follow. But success in these conditions isn't automatic. To nail sharp shots when light is scarce or when speed is essential, you need to balance technique, smart settings, and the right lenses.

This chapter will guide you through the process of capturing clean, sharp images indoors, at night, or during high-speed action—all while making the most of your camera's capabilities.

How to Nail Sharp Shots Indoors and at Night

Indoor and nighttime photography present two major challenges: not enough light and too much motion blur. Here's how to overcome both:

1. **Steady Your Camera:**

   Even a slight shake is exaggerated at slow shutter speeds. Brace yourself against a wall, kneel for stability, or use a tripod/monopod when possible.

2. **Use Faster Shutter Speeds for Moving Subjects:**

   At a wedding reception or indoor sports event, a shutter speed of at least 1/125s is needed to freeze casual movement, and 1/500s or more for athletes in motion.

3. **Open the Aperture Wide:**

   A wide aperture (f/1.8–f/2.8) lets in more light, brightening the shot and blurring backgrounds beautifully.

4. **Leverage Auto ISO:**

   Set a maximum ISO you're comfortable with (such as 6400)

and let the camera adjust as needed to keep exposure balanced.

5. **Seek Out the Light:**

Position subjects near windows, lamps, or streetlights at night. The D850 captures available light well—use it to your advantage.

With practice, you'll learn that night shots aren't about avoiding shadows—they're about learning to work with them.

Best ISO Ranges for Clean Results

The D850's sensor is surprisingly clean even at high ISOs, but every stop introduces some noise. Here's a safe guideline:

- **ISO 64–400:** Virtually noise-free. Use in daylight or well-lit interiors.

- **ISO 800–1600:** Still very clean, excellent for indoor portraits or evening light.

- **ISO 3200–6400:** Acceptable for low light and fast action. Noise is visible but manageable with post-processing.

- **ISO 12,800+:** Emergency use only. Expect heavy grain and loss of detail, but sometimes the shot is worth it.

Tip: Always expose slightly brighter if possible (without blowing highlights). Lifting shadows in editing creates more noise than slightly reducing exposure from a bright capture.

Motion Freezing vs Creative Blur: Using Shutter Speeds Effectively

Shutter speed isn't just technical—it's artistic. It decides whether movement is frozen or shown as motion.

- **Motion Freezing:**

  Use fast shutter speeds to capture sharp action.

  - Sports: 1/1000–1/2000s.

  - Kids running: 1/500–1/1000s.

- o Concert performers: 1/250–1/500s (higher if lighting allows).

- **Creative Blur:**

Sometimes blur tells the story better.

- o Waterfalls or rivers: 1/4–1s for silky effect (tripod essential).

- o Night traffic: 5–30s for light trails.

- o Dance performances: 1/15–1/30s to show graceful motion while keeping faces semi-sharp.

The beauty of the D850 is that its large sensor and dynamic range give you room to experiment.

Lenses That Shine for Low Light

A camera is only as good as the glass in front of it. For low light and action, fast lenses are essential.

- **50mm f/1.8G or f/1.4G:** Affordable, sharp, and great for portraits or indoor candids.

- **85mm f/1.8G:** A classic portrait lens—bright and flattering, even in dim reception halls.

- **24–70mm f/2.8E VR:** Versatile zoom for events, with constant f/2.8 aperture and stabilization.

- **70–200mm f/2.8E FL VR:** The workhorse for sports, concerts, and weddings, balancing reach with speed.

- **35mm f/1.8G:** Perfect for environmental portraits and street photography at night.

These lenses not only gather more light but also produce shallower depth of field, which helps isolate subjects in busy environments.

How to Reduce Noise While Keeping Detail

Noise is the price of higher ISOs, but there are ways to control it:

1. **Expose to the Right (ETTR):** Slightly overexpose (without clipping highlights) so that shadows aren't crushed. Darkening in post introduces less noise than brightening.

2. **Use Fast Glass:** A wider aperture reduces the need for high ISO in the first place.

3. **Enable High ISO Noise Reduction:** The D850 allows in-camera noise reduction, though it can soften details. Use it moderately.

4. **Post-Processing:** Software like Lightroom or DxO PhotoLab has excellent noise-reduction tools that preserve detail while smoothing grain.

5. **Shoot RAW:** Noise is far easier to manage in RAW files than in JPEGs.

Noise reduction isn't about eliminating every grain—it's about striking a balance so your images look natural and detailed.

Cheat Sheet: Low Light & Action Settings at a Glance

- **Indoor Portraits:** f/2.8, 1/125s, ISO 800–1600, single-point AF on the eye.

- **Concerts:** f/2.8, 1/250s, Auto ISO up to 6400, AF-C with Group Area.

- **Sports Outdoors (day):** f/4–f/5.6, 1/1000–1/2000s, Auto ISO.

- **Sports Indoors:** f/2.8, 1/500–1/1000s, ISO 3200–6400, AF-C Dynamic Area.

- **Night Street Photography:** f/1.8–f/2.8, 1/60s handheld, ISO 1600–3200.

- **Light Trails:** f/8–f/11, 10–30s on tripod, ISO 100.

- **Waterfalls (silky effect):** f/11, 1/2–1s on tripod, ISO 64, ND filter optional.

Final Note

Low light and fast action don't have to be intimidating. With the Nikon D850, you have the sensor power and flexibility to handle both gracefully. The key is to know when to prioritize shutter speed, when to open up your aperture, and when to trust higher ISOs. Once you master these, you'll discover that the moments you once missed—whether a candlelit kiss, a soaring basketball dunk, or a city street alive at night—can be captured with clarity, mood, and confidence.

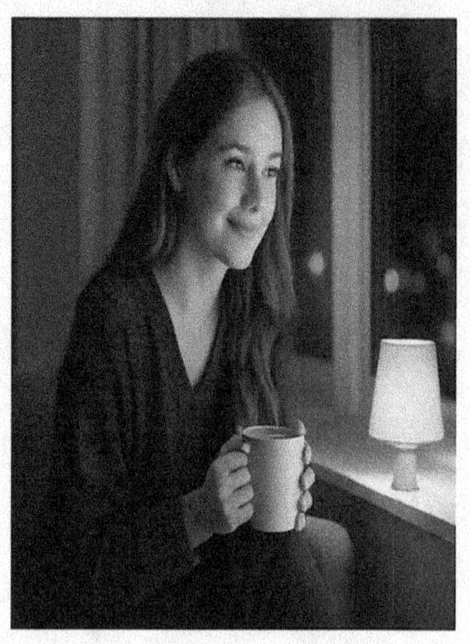

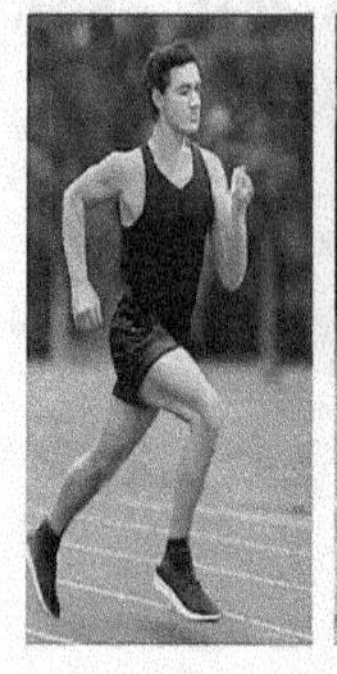
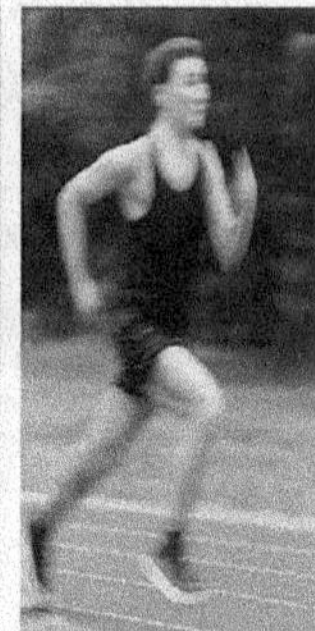

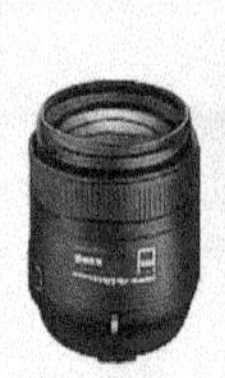
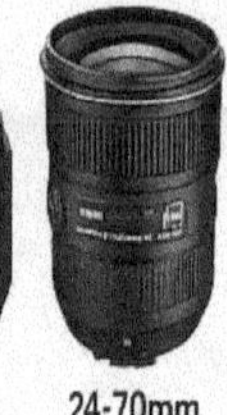

Chapter 6

Unlocking the Power of 4K Video

The Nikon D850 isn't just a stills giant—it's also a surprisingly capable video machine. With full-frame 4K recording, slow-motion options, and high-quality audio inputs, the D850 can stand in for dedicated video cameras when used correctly. That said, video is where the D850 shows both its strengths and its limitations, and knowing these upfront will save you a lot of frustration.

This chapter will guide you through getting set up for 4K, choosing the right frame rates, capturing footage that's easy to edit and grade, and improving audio so your videos don't just look good, but sound professional too.

The D850's Video Strengths (and Weaknesses)

Strengths:

- **Full-Frame 4K Recording:** The D850 captures oversampled, detailed 4K UHD video using the full width of its sensor—perfect for cinematic results.

- **Slow Motion:** In Full HD, you can shoot up to 120 frames per second, creating smooth slow-motion footage.

- **Excellent Dynamic Range:** Just like with stills, the sensor retains highlight and shadow detail, especially when using flat profiles.

- **High-Quality Lenses:** Nikon's F-mount glass provides endless creative options, from ultra-wide landscapes to creamy portrait footage.

- **Audio Options:** Dedicated mic and headphone jacks allow for professional audio monitoring.

Weaknesses:

- **No In-Body Stabilization:** Unlike modern mirrorless cameras, the D850 relies on lens VR or external stabilization (tripods, gimbals).

- **File Size & Heat:** 4K footage creates huge files and can generate heat during long recordings.

- **Autofocus Limitations:** Live View autofocus in video mode can be slower and less reliable than mirrorless competitors. For professional work, manual focus is often more dependable.

Knowing these, you can play to the D850's strengths and work around its shortcomings.

Step-by-Step: Setting Up 4K Recording

1. **Switch to Live View:** Press the LV button near the rear display and toggle to video mode (the little movie camera icon).

2. **Choose Resolution:** In the *Movie Shooting Menu*, set frame size to 3840 × 2160 (4K UHD).

3. **Select Frame Rate:** Pick between 24p, 30p, or 60p depending on your project (explained in the next section).

4. **File Format:** Choose MOV or MP4. MOV offers higher quality, MP4 is more compatible.

5. **Set Picture Profile:** Start with Flat for grading, or Standard if you want straight-out-of-camera footage.

6. **Audio Settings:** In *Movie Sound Settings*, adjust mic sensitivity or select external input.

7. **Stabilization:** If your lens has VR (Vibration Reduction), turn it on for handheld shooting. Otherwise, use a tripod, monopod, or gimbal.

8. **Record:** Press the red movie-record button near the shutter release to start and stop recording.

Choosing Frame Rates (24p, 30p, 60p)

- **24p (24 frames per second):** The "cinematic look." Slightly more motion blur, but it's the industry standard for film-style video. Perfect for storytelling, weddings, and short films.

- **30p (30 frames per second):** Smoother than 24p, commonly used for broadcast, corporate, or YouTube content. A good default if you want a natural look without too much blur.

- **60p (60 frames per second):** Extra smooth motion. Excellent for sports, action, and fast movement. Also useful if you plan to slow footage down to 30p in editing for a half-speed effect.

For ultra-slow motion, switch to 120 fps in Full HD. This won't be 4K, but it allows buttery-smooth slow-motion sequences.

Flat Picture Profiles and Grading Basics

The D850 includes a Flat Picture Control designed for video. It reduces contrast and saturation, keeping as much highlight and shadow detail as possible. This gives you more flexibility in post-production when color grading.

- **Why use Flat?** It prevents harsh blacks and blown-out whites, leaving room to adjust colors later.

- **How to grade:** In editing software (Premiere, DaVinci Resolve, Final Cut), apply a LUT (Look-Up Table) or manually adjust contrast, saturation, and color balance.

- **When to avoid Flat:** If you want quick, shareable footage with no editing, stick to Standard or Neutral. Flat footage looks dull until it's processed.

Think of Flat as a raw canvas—you trade instant punchiness for long-term flexibility.

External Mic Setups for Crisp Audio

Good video ruined by bad audio is still bad video. The built-in D850 mic is serviceable but picks up camera noise and lacks richness. External mics make a huge difference.

- **Shotgun Mic (on-camera):**

    A Rode VideoMic Pro or similar gives focused, directional sound. Great for vlogging or interviews.

- **Lavalier Mic (clip-on):**

  Small mics clipped to clothing, wired or wireless. Perfect for weddings, interviews, and YouTube talking heads.

- **Handheld Mic:**

  Used for presentations or man-on-the-street style recordings.

- **Headphones:**

  Always monitor your audio through the headphone jack to catch issues live.

Tip: Record in quiet environments when possible, and reduce background hum by adjusting mic sensitivity instead of boosting volume later.

Tips for Vloggers, YouTubers, and Wedding Filmmakers

For Vloggers & YouTubers:

- Use a wide lens (24–35mm) to capture yourself at arm's length.

- Mount the camera on a tripod or small gimbal for smoother footage.

- Stick with 30p for a natural look on YouTube.

- Prioritize audio—audiences forgive shaky video but not poor sound.

For Wedding Filmmakers:

- Use dual card slots to ensure backup while recording.

- Switch between 24p for cinematic sequences (ceremony, couple portraits) and 60p for reception dancing or action shots.

- Always carry fast prime lenses (f/1.8 or f/2.8 zooms) to handle low light.

- Capture ambient audio (clapping, laughter, vows) as well as mic'd voices to add atmosphere.

For Event and Documentary Shooters:

- Use monopods for mobility in crowded spaces.

- Record in Flat to give yourself more grading options in mixed lighting.

- Don't rely heavily on autofocus—manual focus ensures consistent results during speeches or interviews.

Final Word

The D850 may not be a dedicated cinema camera, but with thoughtful setup, it delivers stunning 4K that rivals modern mirrorless options. Its strengths—full-frame detail, dynamic range, and lens options—make it perfect for storytelling, whether you're creating YouTube videos, documenting weddings, or producing short films. Pair it with good audio, careful stabilization, and smart frame-rate choices, and your footage will look professional, polished, and timeless.

Strengths (and Weakensses)

- Full-Frame 4K Recording
- Slow Motion
- Excellent Dynamic Range
- High-Quality Lenses
- Audio Options

Choosing Frame Rates (24p, 30p, 60p)

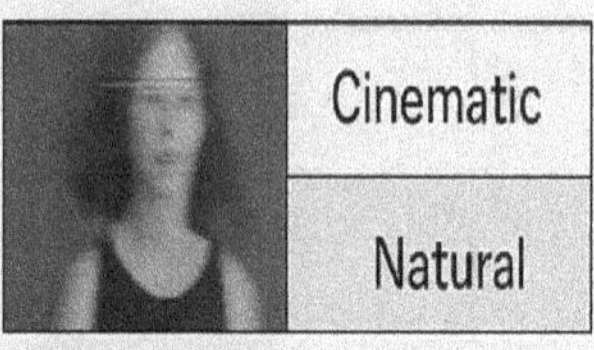

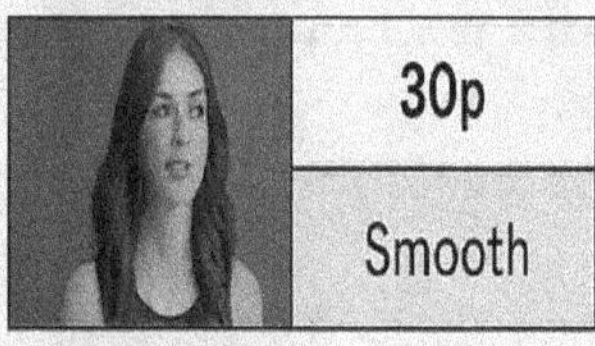

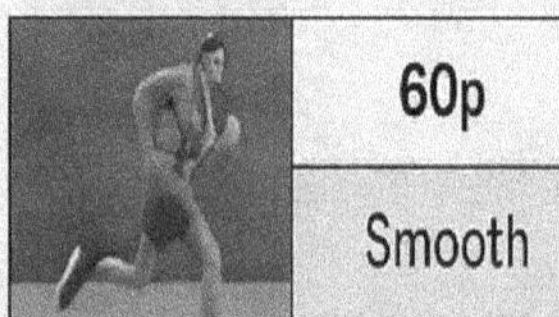

Extornal Mic Setups for Crisp Audio

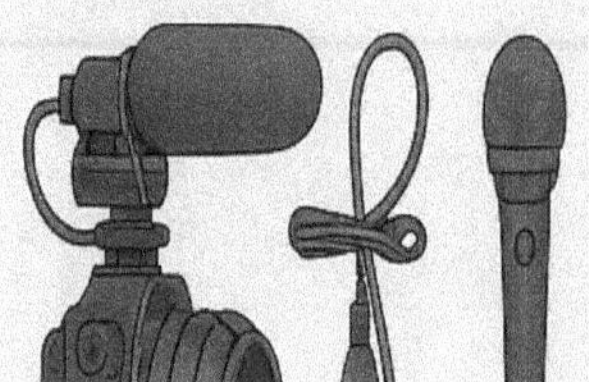

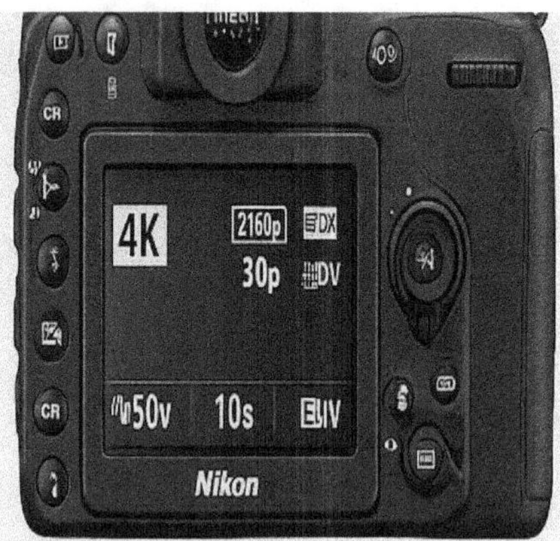

Step-by-Step: Setting Up 4K Recording

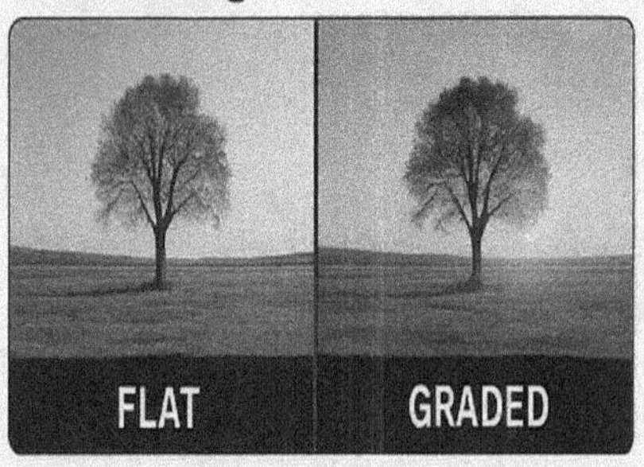

Tips for Vloggers, YouTubers, and Wedding Filmmakers

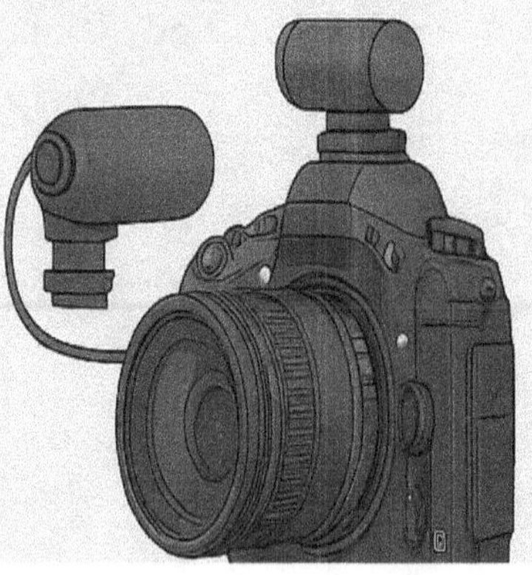

Chapter 7

Lenses & Accessories That Transform Your D850

The Nikon D850 is a phenomenal body, but it doesn't reach its true potential until you pair it with the right lenses and accessories. Think of the camera as the engine and your lenses and gear as the tires, suspension, and steering—without them, the ride won't feel complete. In this chapter, we'll explore the lenses that truly unlock the D850's power, the accessories that add real value, and how to make smart choices without drowning in marketing-driven "must-haves."

Best Lens Choices for Portraits, Landscapes,

Wildlife, and Macro

Portrait Lenses

Portraits demand lenses that flatter faces, produce beautiful background blur (bokeh), and handle low light gracefully.

- **Nikon 85mm f/1.8G or f/1.4G:** Classic portrait lenses. The f/1.8 is affordable and sharp, while the f/1.4 offers creamier background separation.

- **Nikon 70–200mm f/2.8E FL VR:** A versatile zoom for weddings and events, perfect for headshots and full-body portraits alike.

- **Nikon 50mm f/1.8G:** Lightweight, inexpensive, and wonderful for environmental portraits with natural perspective.

Landscape Lenses

Landscapes call for wide fields of view, edge-to-edge sharpness, and the ability to shoot at narrower apertures for depth.

- **Nikon 14–24mm f/2.8G:** An ultra-wide classic for dramatic skies, sweeping mountains, and interiors.

- **Nikon 24–70mm f/2.8E VR:** The go-to standard zoom for everything from landscapes to travel, offering flexibility without changing lenses.

- **Nikon 20mm f/1.8G:** Lightweight, wide, and sharp—great for night skies and astro photography.

Wildlife Lenses

Wildlife photography demands reach, fast autofocus, and stabilization.

- **Nikon 200–500mm f/5.6E VR:** A budget-friendly super-telephoto, sharp and surprisingly portable.

- **Nikon 500mm f/5.6E PF ED VR:** Lightweight for its reach, perfect for birds and distant subjects.

- **Nikon 70–200mm f/2.8E FL VR:** Shorter reach but versatile for zoos, safaris, and sports.

Macro Lenses

Macro reveals the hidden world of close-ups—flowers, insects, jewelry, textures.

- **Nikon 105mm f/2.8G VR Micro:** The gold standard for macro, with stabilization and working distance.

- **Nikon 60mm f/2.8G Micro:** Great for product photography and studio setups where you can get closer.

Remember: the best lens is the one that suits your shooting style, not necessarily the one with the highest price tag.

Tripods, Filters, and Flashes That Actually Add

Value

Tripods

The D850's resolution is unforgiving of camera shake. A sturdy tripod is essential for landscapes, night photography, or long exposures.

- **Carbon Fiber Tripods:** Lightweight yet stable for travel and hiking.

- **Aluminum Tripods:** Heavier, but affordable and durable for studio or home use.

- **Ball Heads:** Allow smooth and flexible adjustments.

Filters

Filters can expand creative options in ways editing alone can't.

- **Polarizing Filters:** Reduce reflections, deepen skies, and make colors pop.

- **Neutral Density (ND) Filters:** Cut light, enabling slow shutter speeds for waterfalls, rivers, and light trails even in daylight.

- **UV Filters:** Mostly protection for your lens glass—choose high quality to avoid image degradation.

Flashes

Natural light is beautiful, but flash gives you control.

- **Nikon SB-700 or SB-5000 Speedlights:** Reliable, powerful flashes with TTL (through-the-lens) metering.

- **Diffusers/Softboxes:** Soften the harshness of flash, creating more natural-looking light.

- **Off-Camera Flash Systems:** For creative lighting setups in portraits or events.

Battery Grips and Storage Tips for Long

Shoots

Battery Grip

The D850 already has good battery life, but long weddings, sports, or wildlife sessions can drain power quickly. A battery grip provides:

- **Extended Battery Life:** Holds a second battery for double the shooting time.

- **Vertical Grip:** Makes portrait orientation more comfortable.

- **Better Balance:** Helps counterbalance large telephoto lenses.

Storage

High-resolution RAW files eat space. A smart storage workflow saves frustration.

- **Use Dual Cards:** Put RAWs on an XQD/CFexpress card and JPEGs on an SD card for redundancy.

- **Offload Regularly:** Carry a portable SSD or laptop on long trips.

- **Organize:** Use labeled card wallets to separate full and empty cards.

Recommended Camera Bags and Straps to Handle Weight

The D850 isn't a lightweight body, and paired with heavy lenses, comfort becomes essential.

Camera Bags

- **Backpacks:** Best for long hikes or travel. Look for padded compartments and weather resistance.

- **Messenger Bags:** Ideal for street and event photography— quick access, less bulky.

- **Rolling Cases:** For pros carrying multiple bodies, lenses, and lighting gear.

Straps

- **Crossbody Straps (like BlackRapid):** Spread the weight and make carrying heavy gear comfortable.

- **Harness Systems:** Distribute weight across shoulders and back—great for event photographers carrying two bodies.

- **Wrist Straps:** Minimalist and light, good for casual outings with smaller lenses.

Avoiding Gear Bloat—What You Really Need vs Marketing Hype

The photography industry thrives on convincing you that you *need* more. Truth is, most photographers only use a fraction of their gear. Here's how to cut through the noise:

- **Don't chase focal length overlap.** If you own a 24–70mm, you don't *need* a 28–300mm "just in case."

- **Buy lenses for your subjects.** Portrait shooter? Invest in a fast prime. Wildlife enthusiast? Go for reach.

- **Quality over quantity.** Three excellent lenses will serve you better than a dozen mediocre ones.

- **Accessories should solve problems, not collect dust.** A tripod is essential for landscapes; it's useless if you only shoot handheld portraits.

The D850 is already more camera than most people need. Equip it with the right tools for *your* style, and you'll spend more time shooting and less time hauling unused gear.

Closing Thought

The Nikon D850 is a workhorse, but it becomes a creative powerhouse when paired with the right lenses and accessories. Choose gear strategically—let your photography style dictate what you buy, not glossy ads. With a carefully curated kit, you'll be able to handle anything from intimate portraits to vast landscapes, from tiny insects to soaring eagles, without feeling weighed down or overwhelmed.

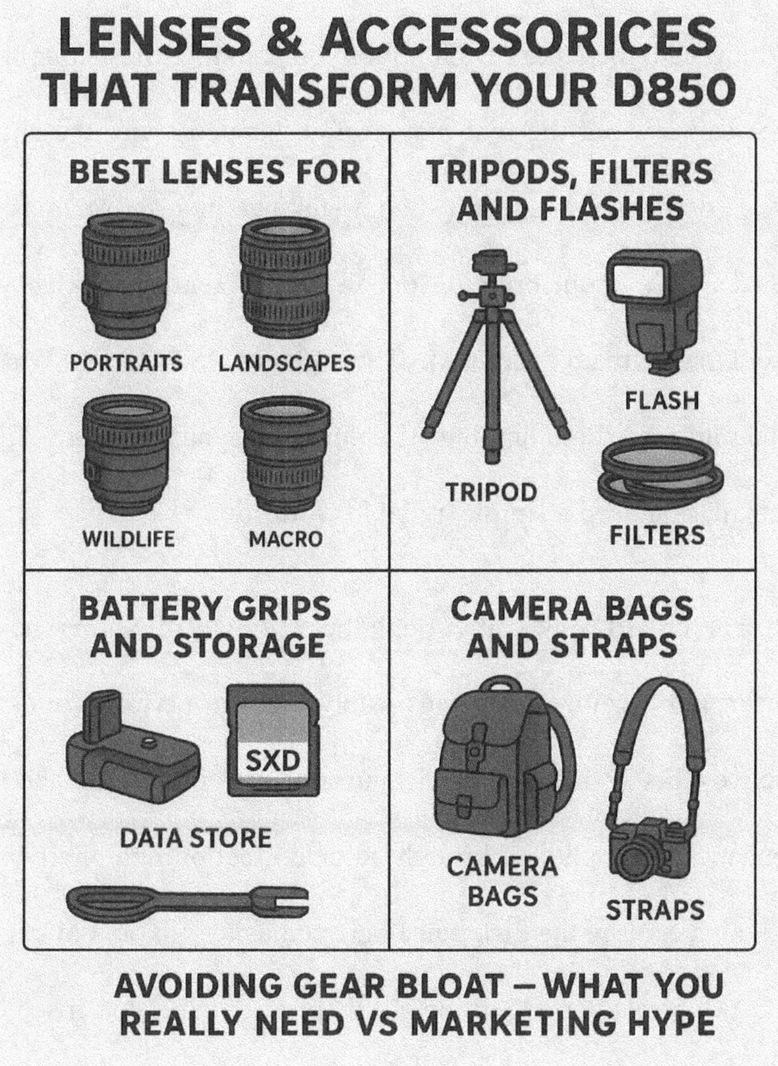

Chapter 8

Post-Processing Made Simple

Shooting with the Nikon D850 gives you stunning files straight out of the camera, but the real magic often happens after the shutter click. Post-processing isn't about faking images or masking mistakes—it's about bringing out the full potential of what your camera has already captured. The D850's 45.7MP RAW files contain an incredible amount of detail and dynamic range, but to unlock it, you need a simple, reliable workflow.

This chapter will walk you through the essentials of editing: how to transfer and organize your files safely, how to perform quick but effective edits in software like Lightroom or Capture One, and how to enhance your photos through color correction and sharpening. We'll also explore the difference between using Nikon's in-camera Picture Controls versus editing RAW files. Finally, you'll see how subtle adjustments can transform a flat image into something that truly sings.

Editing Workflow: Transferring, Organizing, and Backing Up Files

Good editing starts long before you open your photos in software—it begins with how you handle your files. A messy workflow leads to lost images, corrupted cards, or endless hunting through folders. Here's a streamlined approach:

1. **Transfer Safely**

    o Always use a card reader rather than plugging your camera directly into your computer. It's faster and reduces wear on the camera ports.

    o Copy files to a dedicated folder labeled with the shoot date and event name (e.g., "2025-09-02_Wedding_Sam&Lila").

2. **Organize Immediately**

o   Create a master folder for each year. Inside, sort shoots by date and subject.

o   Within each shoot folder, make subfolders: *RAW*, *Exports*, *Edits*. Keep your originals untouched in RAW.

3. **Backup Religiously**

o   Use the 3-2-1 rule: three copies, two different storage types, one off-site (cloud or external).

o   External SSDs are perfect for fast editing storage; cloud storage like Google Drive or Backblaze adds security.

This workflow ensures your D850 files are safe, accessible, and never lost in the chaos.

Quick-Start Editing in Lightroom/Capture

One

Both *Adobe Lightroom* and *Capture One* are excellent platforms for working with D850 RAW files. They're designed to handle large volumes of images efficiently, with tools that make editing intuitive.

- **Import:** Bring your files into the catalog, apply keywords or tags (e.g., "portraits," "landscape," "macro") to keep things searchable.

- **Cull Quickly:** Use flags, stars, or color labels to separate keepers from throwaways. Don't waste time editing rejects.

- **Basic Adjustments:** Start with exposure, contrast, highlights, shadows, and white balance. These five sliders alone can transform most images.

- **Presets/Styles:** Both Lightroom and Capture One allow presets. Use them as starting points, but always fine-tune for each image.

Tip: Work on a calibrated monitor if possible. The D850 captures subtle tones and colors that you want to see accurately.

Color Correction and Sharpening for D850 Files

The D850's files are rich, but they often need refinement to match your vision.

- **Color Correction:**
    - Adjust White Balance first—indoors, images can look too orange; outdoors, too blue.
    - Use the HSL (Hue, Saturation, Luminance) panel to fine-tune specific colors. Make skies deeper, greens more natural, or skin tones more flattering.
    - Watch out for over-saturation—natural tones always look stronger than neon colors.

- **Sharpening:**

  The D850 captures immense detail, but RAW files often
  look soft by design.

  - o Apply sharpening carefully: increase clarity and
    detail, but avoid halos around edges.

  - o Use selective sharpening: apply more to eyes, hair,
    or textures, less to smooth areas like skin.

  - o For web exports, moderate sharpening works best;
    for prints, slightly stronger sharpening is often
    required.

Using Nikon Picture Controls vs RAW Editing

The D850 offers Picture Controls like Standard, Vivid, Neutral, and
Flat. These settings apply directly to JPEGs and influence how the
preview looks on the back of your camera.

- **Picture Controls (In-Camera JPEGs):**

  Great if you want ready-to-use files without editing. Vivid

for landscapes, Portrait mode for flattering skin, Flat if you
plan light grading.

- **RAW Editing:**

RAW files ignore Picture Controls (except as a preview).
This means you can apply your own color styles, contrast,
and sharpening later in software without losing quality.

Which to use?

- If you want speed and convenience, stick with Picture
Controls and JPEGs.

- If you want maximum flexibility and quality, shoot RAW
and edit.

Many photographers do both: RAW + JPEG, getting instant
shareable files alongside deep, editable negatives.

Before & After Examples to Show What's

Possible

Imagine this: you photograph a wedding couple under a tree at sunset. Straight out of the camera, the sky looks a little flat, the couple's faces are slightly in shadow, and the colors are muted.

- **Before:** The RAW file looks good but uninspiring—low contrast, slightly underexposed faces.
- **After:** By lifting shadows, warming the white balance, and adding gentle sharpening, the sky glows golden, the couple's faces are clear, and the entire image feels alive.

Another example: a night street scene.

- **Before:** The RAW file looks dark and noisy.
- **After:** By reducing noise, adjusting highlights, and adding a touch of vibrance, the scene now glows with atmosphere while keeping detail in both bright streetlights and dark alleyways.

These small adjustments don't "fake" the photo—they reveal the richness already inside your D850 files.

Closing Thought

Post-processing is where you shape your images into your personal vision. The Nikon D850 gives you a sensor capable of staggering detail and dynamic range, but it's only when you take control of editing that your photos become more than snapshots. With a safe workflow, a few basic adjustments, and the confidence to experiment, you'll discover that editing is not a chore—it's the second half of photography.

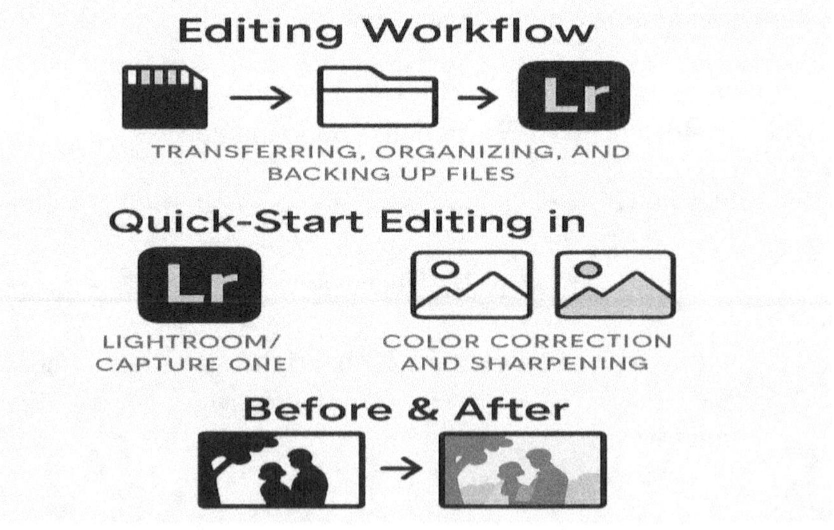

Chapter 9

Custom Buttons, Shortcuts & Pro Handling

The Nikon D850 is a beast of a camera, but left in its default state, it can feel a little slow to navigate. Digging through menus every time you want to change ISO, adjust metering, or swap focus modes wastes valuable seconds—and sometimes costs you the shot. That's why custom buttons and shortcuts matter. They let you tailor the D850 to fit your personal shooting style, so the camera becomes an extension of your eye and hand, not a puzzle you need to solve mid-shoot.

This chapter will show you how to assign buttons for speed, handle the D850 comfortably on long days, and carry it in ways that reduce fatigue. By the end, you'll be able to set up pro-level customizations in minutes and shoot faster, smarter, and with less strain.

Making the D850 Work Faster for Your Shooting Style

Every photographer shoots differently. A wedding photographer needs instant control over ISO for changing light. A wildlife shooter may want fast access to Group-Area AF. A studio portrait photographer may prioritize metering and white balance. The beauty of the D850 is that almost every button, dial, and switch can be reassigned to match your habits.

The goal is to reduce the gap between *seeing the shot* and *capturing it*. If you frequently adjust something, assign it to a button. If you never use a feature, don't waste valuable space on it.

How to Assign Custom Buttons for ISO,

Metering, AF Modes

The D850 offers several buttons you can reprogram: Fn1, Fn2, AE-L/AF-L, Preview, and the joystick (sub-selector). Here's how to use them wisely:

- **ISO on a Button:**

  Assign ISO to the Fn1 or Preview button. Now, while holding that button, you can roll the front dial to adjust ISO instantly. No more menu diving.

- **Metering Mode Shortcut:**

  If you often switch between Matrix, Center-weighted, and Spot metering, assign metering to the Fn2 button. Perfect for event photographers moving between tricky lighting conditions.

- **AF Mode/Area Switch:**

  Wildlife and sports shooters benefit from assigning AF-area mode to a custom button. With one press, you can toggle between Single Point, Group, or Dynamic AF.

- **Sub-Selector Press:**

  That small joystick used to move focus points can also be set to activate AF or recall a stored focus point. Great for quickly locking onto a pre-framed subject (e.g., the finish line at a race).

- **AE-L/AF-L Button:**

  Many pros reassign this button to act as back-button focus if they don't use the dedicated AF-ON button. It's a handy redundancy option.

The key is consistency. Once you assign a button, train your muscle memory until you can hit it without thinking.

Ergonomic Handling Tips for Long Shoots

The D850 is solid, but it's not light. Over time, poor handling leads to sore wrists, stiff shoulders, or even back pain. Professional photographers learn to handle heavy cameras the way athletes learn proper form.

- **Grip Correctly:** Wrap your right hand firmly around the camera grip, but don't strangle it. Use your left hand under the lens barrel to support the weight—this spreads the load and steadies the shot.

- **Balance Large Lenses:** If you're shooting with a 70–200mm or larger telephoto, mount the lens to the tripod, not the camera body. This keeps the balance centered and reduces strain.

- **Adjust Your Posture:** Keep elbows tucked to your sides for stability. Avoid "chicken wings," which fatigue arms quickly.

- **Use the Vertical Grip:** A battery grip not only extends power but makes vertical shooting far more natural and balanced.

Good ergonomics allow you to shoot longer without fatigue and maintain sharpness in your images.

Tricks for Carrying the D850 Without Fatigue

Carrying the D850 for hours—on hikes, at weddings, or during travel—can become a workout in itself. A few smart gear choices can make all the difference:

- **Cross-Body Straps (like BlackRapid):** Sling across your chest, letting the camera rest at your hip. This distributes weight and makes lifting the camera fast and fluid.

- **Harness Systems:** For event shooters with two cameras, harnesses distribute weight evenly across both shoulders and back, preventing neck pain.

- **Wrist Straps:** If you're working light with a prime lens, a wrist strap offers security without bulk.

- **Clip Systems (like Peak Design Capture):** Attach your camera to a belt or backpack strap for hands-free carrying during hikes.

- **Rolling Cases for Travel:** When transporting multiple lenses and bodies, roll instead of carry. Save your strength for the shoot, not the airport.

Even small adjustments—switching from a neck strap to a cross-body strap—can dramatically reduce fatigue after a long day.

Cheat Sheet: Pro-Level Customizations in 10 Minutes

Here's a quick setup you can do right now to transform your D850 workflow:

1. **Fn1 Button → ISO**

   Hold Fn1 + roll dial to adjust ISO instantly.

2. **Fn2 Button → Metering Mode**

   Toggle between Matrix, Spot, and Center-weighted in a second.

3. **Sub-Selector Press → Focus Point Recall**

   Jump to a saved focus point for pre-framed shots.

4. **AF-ON Button → Back-Button Focus**

Separate focus from shutter button for ultimate control.

5. **Preview Button → Depth-of-Field Preview or White Balance Access**

Choose whichever you use more often.

6. **Set My Menu for Fast Access:** Add Format Card, ISO Sensitivity Settings, and Auto Bracketing.

7. **Battery Grip Installed:** Extra battery + vertical grip comfort.

8. **Cross-Body Strap Attached:** Camera at the hip, ready without strain.

In just ten minutes, you'll have turned the D850 into a faster, more responsive machine that matches your personal style.

Closing Thought

Cameras don't make great photos—photographers do. But when you customize your D850 to fit your hands, your instincts, and your shooting style, it becomes invisible. Instead of fighting menus and fumbling for buttons, you'll be free to focus on the story in front of you. And that's the difference between a technically competent shot and a photograph that feels alive.

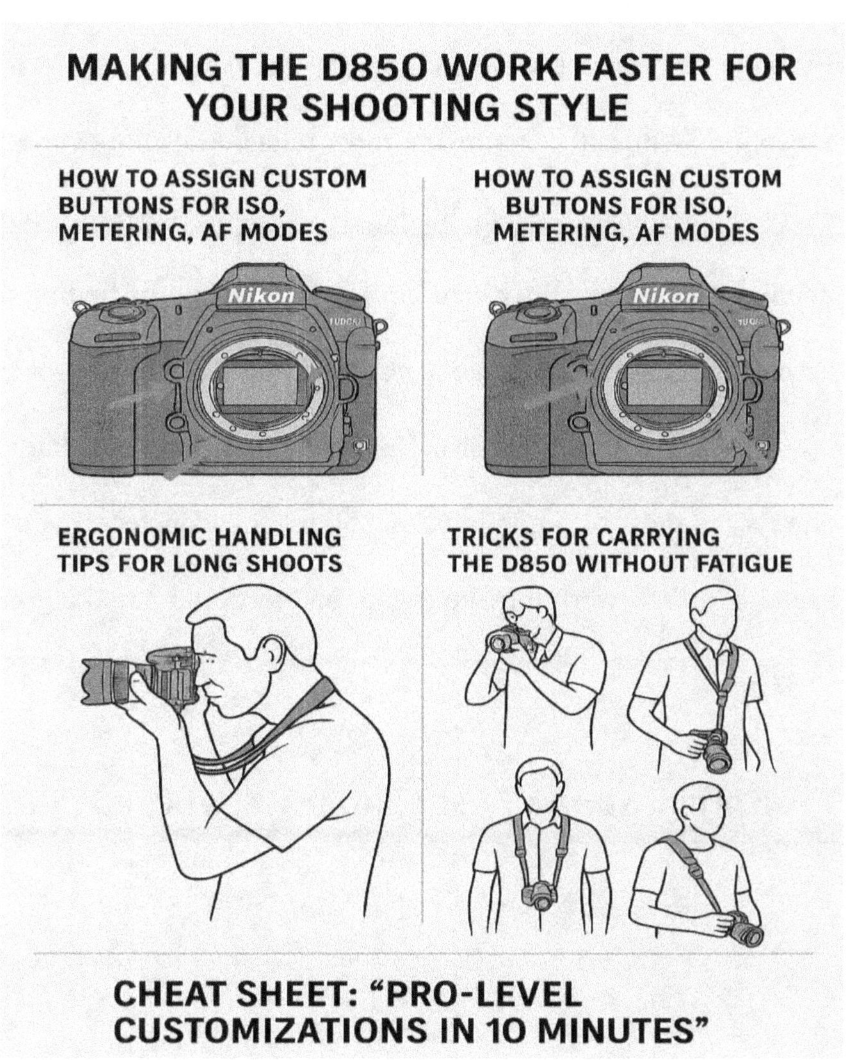

Chapter 10

Common Problems & Quick Fixes

Even the best cameras have their quirks, and the Nikon D850 is no exception. While it's one of the most reliable DSLRs ever built, every photographer eventually faces issues—whether it's blurry photos, stubborn memory card errors, or the dread of finding dust specks on your sensor. The good news is that most of these problems have quick, practical solutions. This chapter will help you diagnose and fix the most common issues D850 users encounter so you can spend less time worrying about gear and more time making great images.

Blurry Shots: Is It Camera Shake, AF, or

Lens?

Few things are as frustrating as reviewing your images only to find that they're soft or blurry. With the D850's massive 45.7MP sensor, even the tiniest shake or focus slip is magnified. To fix the problem, you first need to figure out the cause.

- **Camera Shake:**

  If the whole frame looks smeared, it's likely motion blur from hand-holding. Use the "1 over focal length" rule: if you're shooting at 200mm, keep shutter speed at least 1/200s (preferably faster). Turn on lens VR (Vibration Reduction) if available, and brace your stance for stability.

- **Autofocus Issues:**

  If some parts of the image are sharp but your subject isn't, AF settings may be at fault. For portraits, always place the AF point on the near eye. For moving subjects, use AF-C with Dynamic or Group-Area modes.

- **Lens Quality or Settings:**

Not all blur is operator error—sometimes it's the lens. At very wide apertures (like f/1.4), depth of field can be razor thin. Stopping down slightly to f/2.8 or f/4 often improves sharpness.

Quick Fix Checklist:

1. Raise shutter speed.

2. Use AF mode suited to subject movement.

3. Stop down aperture if depth of field is too shallow.

4. Use a tripod or VR when needed.

Memory Card Errors and How to Avoid Them

The D850's high-resolution files are demanding, and not all memory cards keep up. Occasionally, you may encounter "card error" messages or corrupted files.

- **Use the Right Cards:** Always use XQD/CFexpress or UHS-II SD cards from reputable brands (SanDisk, Sony, Lexar). Avoid cheap, unbranded cards.

- **Format in Camera:** After backing up your photos, format your cards inside the D850 rather than on a computer. This ensures compatibility.

- **Don't Remove Too Soon:** Never pull the card out while the red access light is blinking—it means files are still being written.

- **Replace Old Cards:** Memory cards have lifespans. If one starts acting up, retire it immediately.

If you do get an error, stop shooting, back up what you can, and reformat. Continuing to use a failing card risks losing irreplaceable images.

Battery Drain: How to Extend Life

The D850 has excellent battery performance, but long shoots, cold weather, or heavy use of Live View can drain it faster than expected.

- **Turn Off Image Review:** Constantly showing images after each shot eats power. Disable automatic review if you don't need it.

- **Reduce Live View Usage:** The LCD and sensor drain batteries quickly. Use the optical viewfinder whenever possible.

- **Lower Display Brightness:** Keep the rear screen brightness at a reasonable level.

- **Airplane Mode:** If you use SnapBridge (Bluetooth), turn on Airplane Mode when not transferring files.

- **Carry Spares or Use a Grip:** Extra batteries or a vertical grip with dual batteries ensure you'll never run dry during important shoots.

In cold weather, keep batteries warm in your pocket and rotate them. Lithium-ion batteries lose efficiency in the cold but often "recover" once warmed up.

Overheating in Long Video Sessions

While the D850 isn't known for major overheating issues, extended 4K recording or hot environments can cause the camera to warm up and sometimes shut down.

- **Watch Recording Limits:** The D850's maximum continuous recording time is around 29 minutes. Break long sessions into chunks to avoid heat buildup.

- **Use External Recorders:** HDMI output to a device like an Atomos Ninja reduces internal processing load.

- **Avoid Direct Sun:** Shade your camera during outdoor shoots. A camera baking in full sunlight heats up fast.

- **Turn Off Between Takes:** Give the sensor and processor a breather when possible.

If overheating does occur, power down, remove the battery, and let the camera cool. Pushing it risks damage.

Dust on Sensor—What to Do Safely

Few things frustrate photographers more than discovering dust spots across their skies or portraits. Because of the D850's high resolution, even tiny specks show up clearly.

- **Prevention First:** Always change lenses with the camera turned off (reduces static charge on the sensor). Keep the body facing downward during swaps to avoid dust falling in.

- **Use the Self-Cleaning Function:** The D850 has a built-in sensor cleaning cycle. Run it from the Setup Menu before trying manual methods.

- **Blower Method:** If dust persists, use a manual air blower (never canned air) to puff away particles. Hold the camera with the mount facing down.

- **Wet Cleaning (Last Resort):** If stains remain, use sensor swabs and cleaning fluid specifically designed for full-frame sensors. Move gently in one direction.

- **Professional Service:** If you're uncomfortable cleaning the sensor yourself, take it to a Nikon service center. Better safe than sorry.

Never touch the sensor with your fingers, and never use rough cloths or random cleaning solutions. A careless mistake here can cause permanent damage.

Closing Thought

Problems happen to every photographer—it's part of the process. The difference between frustration and confidence lies in knowing how to respond. With these quick fixes, you'll be prepared to handle the most common challenges of the Nikon D850, from blurry shots to sensor dust. Remember, the D850 is a professional tool built to last, and with a little care and troubleshooting, it will serve you faithfully for years of creative work.

COMMON PROBLEMS & QUICK FIXES

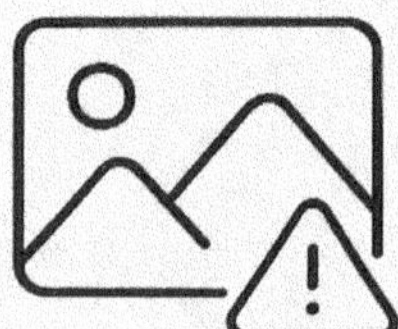

BLURRY SHOTS

- Camera Shake: Faster shutter speed
- AF Issue   Check AF
- Lens Problem   Stop down (e.g. f/8)

MEMORY CARD ERRORS

- Use Proper type (XQD/SD)
- Format in-camera
- Don't remove can.d during access

BATTERY DRAIN

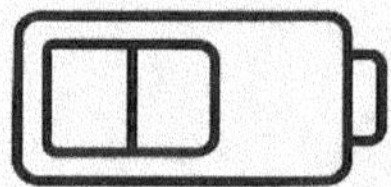

- Turn off Auto Off image review
- Airplane mode
- Lower LCD brightness

OVERHEATING

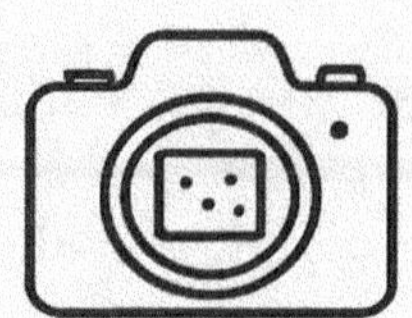

- Reduce recording time
- Use external recorder
- Keep camera cool

DUST ON SENSOR

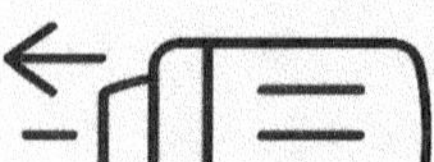

- Clean Images Sensor function
- Use blower

Chapter 11

Practical Shooting Scenarios

The Nikon D850 is versatile enough to handle nearly every type of photography, but the real challenge is knowing which settings and approaches work best for different situations. Instead of memorizing abstract theory, you'll get more value from practical, scenario-based setups you can actually use in the field. This chapter walks you through five of the most common shooting scenarios—portraits, landscapes, wildlife and sports, travel, and weddings/events—and gives you ready-to-apply workflows for each.

Portrait Setup Guide (Studio & Natural Light)

Portraits are about capturing people in a flattering, authentic way. The D850's sensor gives you immense detail, but you need to manage focus, depth of field, and lighting carefully.

Studio Portraits

- **Lens:** 85mm f/1.8 or 70–200mm f/2.8 for flattering compression.

- **Mode:** Aperture Priority (A).

- **Aperture:** f/5.6–f/8 for sharpness across the face.

- **ISO:** 64–200 for maximum image quality under controlled lights.

- **White Balance:** Flash or custom setting matched to your strobes.

- **Focus:** AF-S, Single-Point on the near eye.

Workflow:

Set up soft, even light (softboxes, umbrellas) to avoid harsh shadows. Shoot tethered to a laptop if possible for instant review. For added dimension, use a rim light or hair light behind the subject.

Natural Light Portraits

- **Lens:** 50mm or 85mm prime for shallow depth of field.

- **Aperture:** f/2.8 for creamy background separation.

- **ISO:** Auto, max 1600 for flexibility in changing light.

- **Shutter Speed:** Minimum 1/125s to avoid subject blur.

- **Focus:** AF-C if subject moves; keep point on the eye.

Workflow:

Use shaded areas or golden-hour light for flattering tones. Position your subject so light falls at a gentle angle across the face. If the background is busy, open the aperture for strong separation.

Landscape Setup Guide (Long Exposures, HDR)

Landscapes demand sharpness, depth, and often creative use of long exposures. The D850's dynamic range is perfect for recovering skies and shadows.

- **Lens:** Wide-angle (14–24mm, 20mm, or 24–70mm).

- **Mode:** Manual or Aperture Priority.

- **Aperture:** f/8–f/11 for maximum depth and sharpness.

- **ISO:** 64 for cleanest detail.

- **Focus:** Manual focus or AF-S with focus on 1/3 into the frame (hyperfocal technique).

- **Stability:** Always use a sturdy tripod.

Long Exposures:

For silky waterfalls or night skies, use shutter speeds of 1–30 seconds. Employ ND filters during daylight to slow the shutter.

HDR (High Dynamic Range):

Bracket exposures (e.g., -2, 0, +2 EV) to capture bright skies and dark foregrounds. Merge in software for a balanced result.

Workflow:

Compose carefully, using grid lines for horizons. Take your time—landscapes reward patience. Review histogram to avoid clipped highlights.

Wildlife & Sports Setup Guide

Wildlife and sports share a need for speed, reach, and accuracy. The D850's autofocus system and burst shooting mode excel here.

- **Lens:** 200–500mm f/5.6 for wildlife, 70–200mm f/2.8 for sports.

- **Mode:** Shutter Priority (S) or Manual with Auto ISO.

- **Shutter Speed:** 1/1000s–1/2000s for action; 1/2000s+ for birds in flight.

- **Aperture:** Wide open (f/4–f/5.6) to gather light and isolate subjects.

- **ISO:** Auto, max 6400 to maintain fast speeds.

- **Focus:** AF-C with Dynamic Area (25 points) or Group-Area AF.

- **Drive Mode:** Continuous High for burst sequences.

Workflow:

Track subjects smoothly, keeping your AF points aligned.

Anticipate motion—press the shutter slightly before peak action. Pan with moving subjects for sharp results.

Travel Photography Tips

Travel photography blends portraiture, landscapes, and street photography. The D850 is robust but heavy, so efficiency is key.

- **Lens:** 24–70mm f/2.8 for all-around versatility; 35mm f/1.8 prime for lighter travel.

- **Mode:** Aperture Priority for quick adaptability.

- **Aperture:** f/4–f/8 for most travel scenes.

- **ISO:** Auto, max 3200 for day-to-night coverage.

- **Focus:** AF-S for architecture and static scenes; AF-C for candid street moments.

- **White Balance:** Auto—it handles varied lighting well.

Workflow:

Travel light—carry only what you'll actually use. Use a comfortable strap or clip system for long walks. Back up files daily to an SSD or cloud. Capture both wide establishing shots and close details to tell the story of your journey.

Weddings & Events: Real-World Pro Workflows

Weddings and events are fast-paced, emotional, and often unpredictable. The D850's dual card slots, dynamic range, and autofocus make it a strong choice, but only if you're prepared.

- **Lenses:** 24–70mm f/2.8 for versatility, 70–200mm f/2.8 for ceremonies, 85mm f/1.8 for portraits, and a 35mm f/1.8 for candid storytelling.

- **Mode:** Manual with Auto ISO for consistency across changing lighting.

- **Shutter Speed:** 1/125s for portraits, 1/250s+ for dancing and action.

- **Aperture:** f/2.8–f/4 for portraits, f/5.6+ for group shots.

- **ISO:** Auto with cap at 6400 for receptions.

- **Focus:** AF-C with Group-Area AF for moving subjects; Single Point for posed shots.

- **Backup:** RAWs to XQD, JPEGs to SD for instant delivery/backup.

Workflow:

- Prep: Format cards, carry spares, and pack dual bodies if possible.

- Ceremony: Silent shooting mode for quiet moments, long zoom for distance.

- Reception: Wide prime for atmosphere, fast zoom for action.

- Delivery: Cull quickly, edit for color balance and exposure, deliver both highlight reels and full galleries.

The key to event photography is anticipation. Stay alert, learn to read the flow of moments, and let your customized D850 respond instantly when they unfold.

Closing Thought

The D850 is one of those rare cameras that can handle nearly any scenario with grace, but success isn't about specs—it's about preparation. By setting up your camera with the right lens, exposure choices, and focus modes for each situation, you'll move fluidly from portraits to landscapes, from wildlife to weddings, without hesitation. Photography is about telling stories, and when your technical setup becomes second nature, you'll have more freedom to capture the emotion and meaning behind each scene.

PRACTICAL SHOOTING SCENARIOS

PORTRAIT

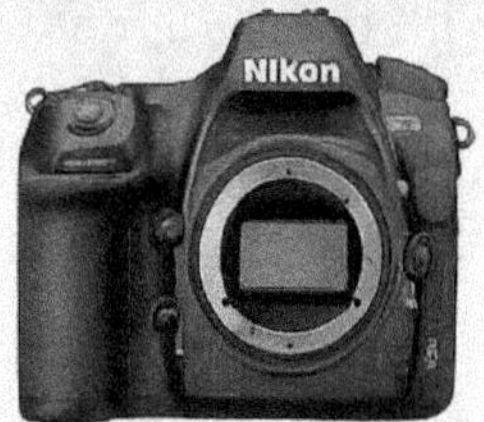

A	A (5.6-5 or F2.aft
ISO	64-200 Auto
AF-S	Single-Point AF

Lens: 85 mm or 50 mm for natul light

LANDSCAPE

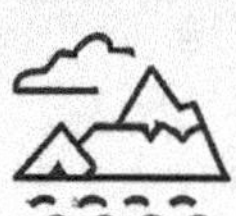

Long Exposures (Long A

	A F/18-f11
ISO 64	A A-F
ISO	AF-Auto
AF-C	Single-Pint AF

Lens: 35 mm or 50 mm for natural

Lens: Telephoto (e.g , 200-500 nm)

WILDLIFE & SPORTS

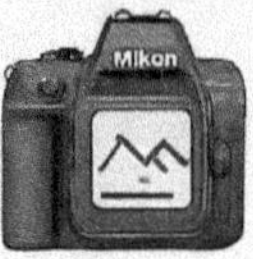

	Shutter Priority or (Auto I50 AutD
	S S/1000-faster
A9	1/4-5.6
ISO	Auto

Lens: Wide-angle (14 - 24 mm, etc.)

TRAVEL

	Monde
	M Auto ISO
SI 1/ 25	S 1/125 of+
AF-S	t/2.8-f5
AF-C	Group-Area AF

Lenss: 24-70 mm or lightweight prime

TRAVEL

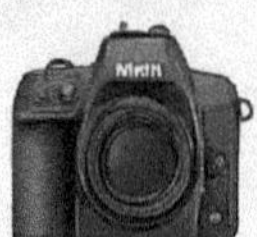

	Amode
	M Auto ISO
	S A/4-8 l
AF-S	Auto

Lens: 24-70 mm or lightweight prime

WEDDINGS & EVENTS

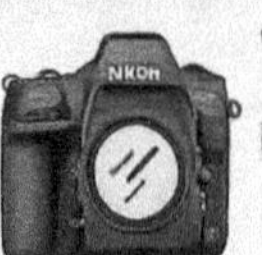

	Weddings & Events
	M Auto ISO
	S 1/125 of+
ISO	f/2,8-f5

Lenses: 24-70 mm, 70-200 mm, 85 mm

Chapter 12

Growing With the D850

Mastering the basics of the Nikon D850 is just the beginning. This camera isn't a tool you "finish learning"—it's one you grow with, adapting its capabilities to your evolving style and ambitions. Whether you're starting out, exploring hybrid setups with drones and gimbals, preparing your work for professional outlets, or simply looking for ways to stay inspired, the D850 has the depth to grow with you. This chapter is about moving from competent operator to confident creator.

From Beginner to Confident Creator

When you first unbox the D850, the sheer number of buttons and menu options can feel overwhelming. But by now, you've learned how to set up, customize, and adapt your camera to fit your style.

The next step is turning that technical comfort into creative confidence.

- **Know Your Defaults:** Have a go-to setup for portraits, landscapes, or action so you can react quickly without second-guessing settings.

- **Experiment with Manual Mode:** Once you understand aperture, shutter speed, and ISO, start experimenting with Manual + Auto ISO or full Manual. This gives you maximum creative control.

- **Review Intentionally:** Instead of checking every image for flaws, review to learn: how's the composition, exposure, and focus? Over time, you'll rely less on the screen and more on instinct.

- **Trust the Process:** The D850 is built to reward practice. The more you shoot, the more second nature it becomes.

Confidence comes not from knowing everything, but from knowing you can figure out anything the camera throws at you.

Using the D850 Alongside Drones, Gimbals, and Mirrorless

Photography today often blends multiple tools. The D850 remains a powerhouse for stills, but pairing it with modern accessories and systems expands what you can create.

- **Drones:** Use drones for aerial perspectives the D850 can't reach. Pair drone wide shots with D850 detail shots for complete storytelling (e.g., landscapes, weddings, real estate).

- **Gimbals:** The D850 lacks in-body stabilization, but a motorized gimbal transforms it into a smooth video machine. Perfect for cinematic wedding sequences, YouTube B-roll, or event coverage.

- **Mirrorless Companions:** If you later add a Nikon Z series body, the D850 makes an excellent second camera. Use the D850 for long battery life and telephoto work, while using mirrorless for lightweight video or eye-detect autofocus.

Instead of seeing newer tools as competition, treat them as companions. The D850 integrates beautifully into a modern hybrid workflow.

Preparing Your Photos for Print, Stock, or Social Media

Your photos aren't finished until they reach an audience. How you prepare them depends on where they're going.

Printing

- **Resolution:** With 45.7MP files, you can print large—poster size or bigger—without losing detail.

- **Sharpening:** Apply slightly more sharpening for print than for web.

- **Color Space:** Export in AdobeRGB or TIFF if working with professional labs.

Stock Photography

- **Clean Files:** Editors reject noisy or over-processed files. Shoot at base ISO whenever possible.

- **Keywords:** Add accurate metadata and descriptions to increase discoverability.

- **Consistency:** Maintain a professional look across your submissions.

Social Media

- **Crop Smart:** Instagram favors 4x5 verticals, while Facebook and Twitter handle 16:9 landscapes well.

- **Compression:** Export JPEGs around 2000–3000px on the long edge to balance quality and upload speed.

- **Style:** Consistency matters more than perfection. Develop a recognizable editing style.

The D850 gives you files rich enough for any platform—you just need to adapt output to the destination.

Staying Inspired: Creative Projects and Challenges

Even with a world-class camera, it's easy to fall into ruts. Inspiration isn't always automatic—it often comes from giving yourself purposeful challenges.

- **Themed Projects:** Dedicate a week to black-and-white portraits, reflections, or street textures.

- **Daily or Weekly Challenges:** One photo a day, or one story a week. Regular shooting builds skill and discipline.

- **Limitations as Creativity Boosters:** Use only one lens for a month, or shoot only at one aperture. Constraints often lead to fresh ideas.

- **Collaborations:** Work with other creatives—models, writers, or filmmakers. The D850's versatility makes it a strong partner across disciplines.

- **Print Your Work:** Seeing your photos in print adds weight and permanence. It pushes you to refine your craft beyond the screen.

The more you challenge yourself, the more the D850 becomes not just a tool, but a partner in your creative journey.

Closing Thought

The Nikon D850 isn't a camera you outgrow—it's a camera you grow into. From first steps as a beginner to professional-level mastery, from handheld portraits to drone-assisted storytelling, from quiet personal projects to large-scale prints, it evolves with you. The key is to keep experimenting, keep learning, and keep creating. As long as you stay curious, the D850 will continue to surprise you with just how much it can do.

Growing with the D850

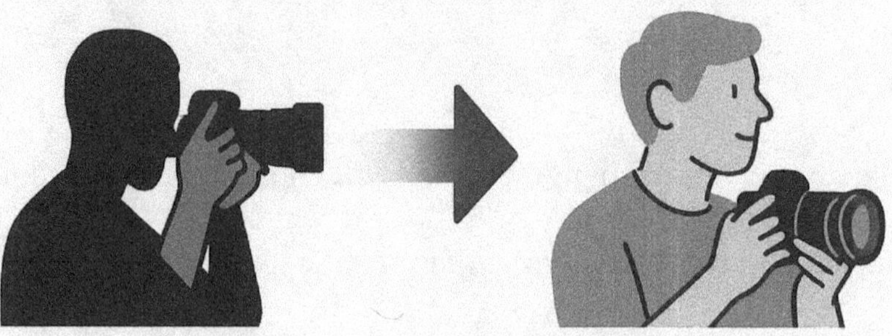

Using the D850 Alongside :

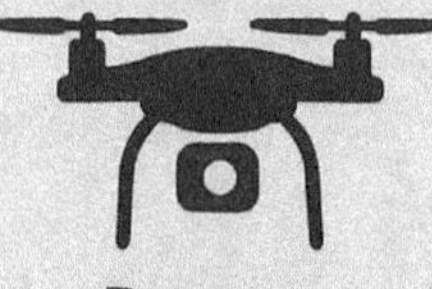
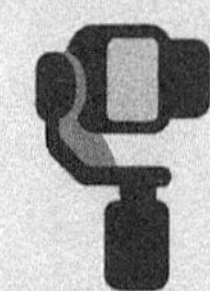
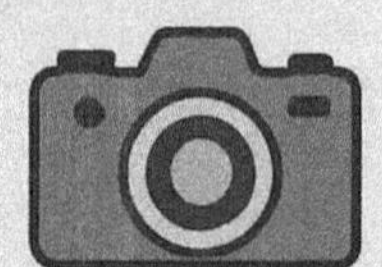

Preparing Your Photos for:

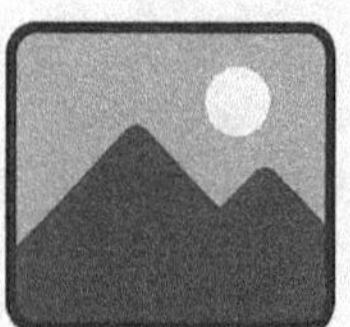
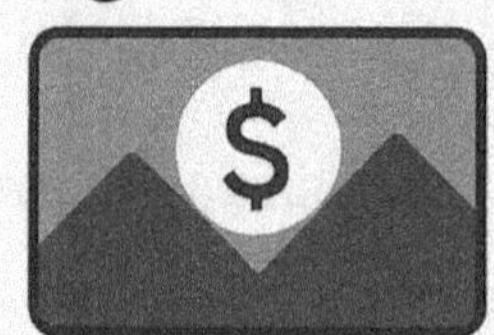

Staying Inspired :

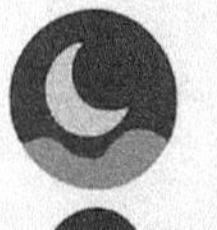
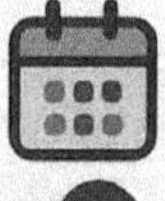

- Themed Projects
- Challenges
- Limitations
- Collaborations

Back Matter

The back matter of this book is designed as your quick-access toolkit. Whether you're on a shoot and need fast settings, want to refresh a photography term, or are looking for communities where you can learn and share, this section has you covered.

Quick Reference Cheat Sheets

When time is short, and you just need to set up quickly, use these cheat sheets. They're designed to give you practical starting points—you can always fine-tune based on lighting and creative intent.

Portraits (studio & natural light)

- Mode: Aperture Priority (A)
- Aperture: f/2.8–f/4 for shallow depth of field
- Shutter: 1/125–1/250s

- ISO: Auto, cap at 1600

- Focus: AF-S, Single-Point on the near eye

Landscapes (daylight & long exposure)

- Mode: Manual or Aperture Priority

- Aperture: f/8–f/11 for sharpness front to back

- Shutter: Variable (tripod for slow exposures)

- ISO: 64 for cleanest files

- Focus: Manual, hyperfocal distance, or AF-S on 1/3 into the frame

Action (sports & wildlife)

- Mode: Shutter Priority or Manual with Auto ISO

- Shutter: 1/1000–1/2000s

- Aperture: f/4–f/5.6

- ISO: Auto, cap at 6400

- Focus: AF-C, Dynamic Area (25 points) or Group-Area

- Drive: Continuous High burst

- Mode: Aperture Priority or Manual with Auto ISO

- Aperture: f/1.8–f/2.8

- Shutter: 1/60s or faster for handheld

- ISO: 1600–6400 (higher if necessary)

- Focus: AF-S or AF-C with center point for reliability

- Tip: Use fast primes and embrace ambient light sources

Glossary of Photography Terms (Plain Language)

Aperture: The opening inside the lens that controls how much light enters the camera. A wide aperture (f/1.8) blurs backgrounds; a narrow aperture (f/11) keeps more in focus.

Autofocus (AF): The system that automatically adjusts the lens to bring subjects into focus.

Back-Button Focus (BBF): A method of focusing by pressing a button on the back of the camera (AF-ON) instead of half-pressing the shutter.

Burst Mode (Continuous Shooting): Taking multiple shots rapidly by holding down the shutter button—useful for sports or action.

Depth of Field: How much of the image (front to back) appears in focus. Controlled mainly by aperture.

Dynamic Range: The ability of the camera to capture detail in both bright highlights and dark shadows in the same shot.

Exposure: The amount of light captured by the sensor, determined by the combination of aperture, shutter speed, and ISO.

ISO: The sensor's sensitivity to light. Low ISO gives cleaner images; high ISO brightens dark scenes but adds noise.

Noise: Grainy or speckled appearance in an image, usually at high ISOs or when brightening shadows too much.

RAW File: An unprocessed digital negative containing maximum detail and flexibility for editing.

Shutter Speed: How long the camera's shutter stays open. Fast speeds freeze motion; slow speeds blur movement.

White Balance: Adjusting colors to make them look natural under different light sources (sun, shade, tungsten, etc.).

Index (by Feature & Shooting Scenario)

Chapter 11

Final Note

This guide was designed to grow with you. Return to the cheat sheets for quick setups, dip into the glossary whenever a term feels unclear, and explore the communities to stay inspired. With the D850 in your hands and the knowledge from these pages, you're equipped not just to take pictures, but to create lasting photographs that carry meaning.

Acknowledgments

No book is ever created in isolation, and this one is no exception. I owe a deep debt of gratitude to the countless photographers—both professionals and passionate beginners—who have shared their experiences, challenges, and questions about the Nikon D850 over the years. Your stories, frustrations, and triumphs are what shaped this guide into something practical and human, rather than just another technical manual.

I would also like to thank the vibrant photography community around the world—those who keep experimenting, sharing tips, and pushing the boundaries of what cameras like the D850 can do. Online forums, workshops, and local meetups have been invaluable sources of real-world insights, far beyond what a product manual could ever provide.

A special note of appreciation goes to the mentors, teachers, and colleagues who encouraged me to see photography not just as a craft, but as a way of seeing the world differently. Your wisdom continues to remind me that the heart behind the lens matters as much as the settings inside it.

Finally, to my readers: thank you for trusting me to be part of your photographic journey. Whether you are picking up the Nikon D850 for the first time or seeking to master its full potential, your curiosity and commitment to learning are the reasons this book exists. It is my sincere hope that the pages ahead will make your path clearer, your work stronger, and your creative vision even more alive.

About The Author

Randy Osborn is a trusted name in the world of camera education, known for transforming complex gear manuals into simple, step-by-step guides that anyone can understand. With over a decade of experience working hands-on with leading camera systems—from Sony and Canon to Nikon, Leica, and more—Randy has helped thousands of photographers, content creators, and everyday users get the most out of their cameras without the overwhelm.

Driven by a passion for accessible learning, Randy creates user-friendly books that strip away the jargon and focus on real-world usage. Whether you're shooting your first vlog, learning manual mode for the first time, or simply trying to take better family photos, Randy's guides are designed to make every setting click.

Each book combines clear instruction, practical tips, and

relatable language, making it easy for beginners and seasoned hobbyists alike to master their gear and capture life with confidence.

When he's not writing, Randy enjoys field testing new camera releases, hosting beginner-friendly workshops, and exploring hidden photography gems across the globe.

Join the journey to sharper skills and smarter shooting— one page at a time.